CW00762364

HORNS (

Edited by Sorita d'Este

Other titles by the same author:

The Isles of the Many Gods
The Guises of the Morrigan
Circle of Fire
Wicca: Magickal Beginnings
Practical Planetary Magick
Practical Elemental Magick
Avalonia's Book of Chakras
Hekate: Keys to the Crossroads (Editor)
Artemis: Virgin Goddess of the Sun & Moon

HORNS OF POWER
Edited by Sorita d'Este

Contributions by:

Brian Andrews, Harry Barron, Stephen Blake,
Dafydd ap Bran, John Canard, Rhys Chisnall, Sorita d'Este,
Nina Falaise, Thea Faye, Gareth Gerrard, Kim Huggens,
Janet Nancy James, Peter J Jaynes, Phil Lightwood-Jones,
Gulia Laini, Magin, Hortus St Michael, Frater Nechesh,
Nic Phillips, Marc Potts, David Rankine, Beth Raven,
Jenny Sumaya, Zachary Yardley, Zagreus

Published by Avalonia
2008

Published by Avalonia

BM Avalonia
London
WC1N 3XX
England, UK

www.avaloniabooks.co.uk

HORNS OF POWER

ISBN (10) 1905297173
ISBN (13) 978-1905297177

First Edition, July 2008

Design by Satori

For Grant.
A black teardrop forever.

TABLE OF CONTENTS

Cornucopia: Myth & History

Wild Hunt: Rites & Experiences

Horns of Beauty: Horned Goddesses

List of Illustrations

'Herne' by Marc Potts

INTRODUCING
The Horns of Power

Horns represent the primal power of nature, expressed through the strength of a bull or the unstoppable power of a charging herd of buffalo or caribou, the majesty and raw virility of a roaring stag with its antlers silhouetted against the morning sun. They also represent the lunar power in the heavens, lighting the night sky and drawing the tides as the moon waxes and wanes. Horns have been synonymous with this strength throughout human history and it is easy to see why horns should have such an enduring and universal appeal.

The mystical symbolism inherent in nature influenced our ancestors, who saw the trees of the forest in the branch-like antlers of a stag, and the crescent moon in the horns of a bull. Horns represented the subtle as well as the manifest, with the spiral horns of the ram suggesting a journey into mystery. These different horns emphasised the union of the divine and the animal, man's path from the past to the future, drawing on both to attain balance and gain the power that they all have to offer.

Horned animal deities played a significant role in the early civilizations of the ancient world, where the majesty, power and mysteries of the bull gods of Sumeria and ram and bull gods of ancient Egypt would be transmitted into the civilizations that would follow and build on the foundations they had laid.

That horns symbolised power in the ancient world is perfectly demonstrated in the tales of Alexander the Great. He was often depicted with horns emphasising his great martial prowess and supremacy as a leader, whilst at the same time hinting at his divine origins and authority. Indeed as a result of this association he was sometimes called *Karnayn* which means *'horned'*.

Gods such as the Greek Pan, the Minoan bull god, the Roman Faunus and the Harappan Pashupati all demonstrate the enduring power, appeal and diversity of the horned gods. The early Jews also celebrated the power of the bull, associated with storms and a natural symbol of the storm god Yahweh, as the horns on the corners of the altar of Moses. Although the Christian Church would subsequently demonise horns as a symbol of evil, Michelangelo hinted at this ancient connection in his famous statue of the horned Moses.

Evidence from thousands of years before civilization of the earliest recorded images and archaeological remains abound with horns. Items made from horn, such as headdresses and helmets, staffs and tools have been found in grave goods dating back many thousands of years. Horned animals such as bulls, bison, ibex and stags are all common in pre-historic cave art, and antlers bedeck the most famous of all cave figures, the *'Sorceror'*, believed to have been created more than 32,000 years ago, in what is now Les Trois-Frères at Ariège in France.

From ancient Sumeria through to the Celts and Vikings, horned helmets were worn as a symbol of ferocity and power. Through an act of sympathetic magick the wearer of the helmet drew on the immense strength and endurance of the bull or other horned beast represented thereon. The same is of course true of other uses of horn in magickal tools from drinking vessels to trumpets to wands.

Before we can continue we need to clarify the difference between horns and antlers. Antlers are bone extrusions which grow from the heads of most species of deer, and are shed annually. Horns are also bony extrusions, but unlike antlers they are covered with the hard protein substance keratin. Horns are not shed, and grow continuously with the addition of new tissue at the base of the horns.

Some instances which do not fit this definition are commonly and inaccurately called horn. For example rhinoceros horn is made only from keratin with no bony core, and the narwhale tusk, so long confused with the horn of the unicorn, is in fact a giant tooth. Keratin itself is the hard structural protein which also forms nails and hairs in humans. The occurrence of keratin in all these types of horn as well as in us humans as a species emphasises the personal connection we all have to the strength and power of horn.

To many people horns represent the image of the horned god. But which horned god exactly? The horns of power manifest in many different ways, relevant to people and the environment they live in. In the twenty-first century, with its ever-expanding urban centres, people are turning back to the primal gods of old to awaken them to the energy of the land and reconnect with that ancient power.

In this anthology essays by a number of scholars, modern day Pagans, bards, artists and other individuals with a special interest in the horned deities of our ancestors are brought together, clearly showing the diversity and widespread belief in these beings in the ancient world as well as providing us with accounts of personal encounters in the here and now. Furthermore, scattered throughout this volume are examples of evocations, invocations and oracles honouring the horned gods throughout history, breaking through the boundaries of time and space. These have been included to inspire and to induce an atmosphere in which the horned deities on these pages can gain a life of their own in the minds and hearts of the readers, singing their song to the sound of distant music and the dance of the beating heart of the wildwood.

In the final section the reader is presented with a few essays considering the divine feminine as being horned, including the horns and horned deities found in the *Greek Magical Papyri*, i.e. the goddesses Hekate, Artemis and Selene, and an experiential journey of a Priestess seeking the antlered goddess Elen. The horned lunar goddess emphasises different types of power to the horned god, but is at least as significant in her dominion. The most obvious indication of this, where the lunar goddess with her crescent horns assumes centre stage, is of course the Wiccan tradition and its many pagan derivatives; some of which also include the horned god.

And so now it is time to hand you, the reader, the cornucopia of knowledge and experience of horned deities that has gathered to the call blown on the horn of convocation, offerings of labour and wisdom inspired by the horns of power.

Sorita d'Este,
June 2008

CONTRIBUTORS

WRITERS & ARTISTS OF HORNS OF POWER

The following individuals gave of their time, energy and creative talent to make this project you hold in your hands a possibility. It is their passion that manifested as *Horns of Power*:

Beth Raven

Beth is passionate about British folklore, the spirits of the land and the Gods of yesterday and today. She is an ordained priestess in the Fellowship of Isis and the founder of the Temple of Medb. She enjoys tending to her garden and hiking, bird watching and indulging in her love of the little people – both in the unseen sense, as well as in her chosen career as a midwife.

Brian Andrews

Artist Brian Andrews is a native of South London, whose interests, outside of art and magick, include comic books, gardening, computer games and playing music. He has contributed articles to magazines such as the Children of Artemis' *Witchcraft & Wicca* and his artwork has featured in *The Guises of the Morrigan; Heka* and *Artemis Virgin Goddess of the Sun & Moon*.

Dafydd ap Bran

Dafydd is a Welsh bard and musician who live in the Snowdonia mountains in Wales. He is passionate about the Pagan religions of the British Isles and can often be found reading and discussing the tales of many of the heroes with friends around a campfire, probably whilst drinking homemade mead.

David Rankine

Esoteric researcher and author David Rankine has a life long fascination for the myths and Gods of the ancient world. He is the author of numerous books on magick, witchcraft and mythology, partnering for projects with his wife Sorita d'Este and with the occult scholar Stephen Skinner. His published works includes *The Isles of the Many Gods, Climbing the Tree of Life, Practical Planetary Magick, Keys to the Gateway of Magic, The Goetia of Dr Rudd* and *the Veritable Key of Solomon*. For more about David and his work see *www.ritualmagick.co.uk*

Frater Nechesh

A devotee of Babalon, Frater Nechesh has trained in a number of systems of western yoga. He is a keen scholar of the unknown, exploring the ancient mythologies through every medium available to him. He holds a post graduate degree in performing arts, which is nice. His life ambition is to wake up one morning as a hairy poet; instead he is bald and continues the search for his Scarlet Woman.

Gareth Gerrard

A scientist by trade, a Witch by inclination and inveterate misser of deadlines, Gareth is a well known speaker at conferences and festivals in the UK. He is passionate about Welsh Gods, Welsh Rugby, and Tea. He is originally from Cardiff (Wales) but now lives in West London with his wife, daughter and fat idiot cat.

Gulia Laini

An initiate of the Western School of Magick, Gulia enjoys reading and researching her family tree. She is currently developing her own unique system of predictive astro-palmistry by merging horary astrology with scientific palmistry.

Harry Barron

As a healer and Wiccan High Priest, both Harry's work and spiritual life are focused around healing and the natural world. Having studied in both London and Shanghai, he currently practices Chinese Medicine and Acupuncture from his practice in Mid-Wales. He is a keen linguist, fluent in several languages and is passionate about cooking vegetarian food. Harry's work was included in the *Hekate Keys to the Crossroads* collection and he is currently researching issues related to Pagan ethics for a book he is writing.

Hortus St Michael

Hortus' interest in the legends of Herne the Hunter developed out of a chance meeting with a likeminded soul in the Bells of Ouseley, a wonderful old public house in Old Windsor, England, many years ago. He is a keen gardener and spends a great deal of his time tending his nearly two acre formal garden, sometimes with the help of his long suffering wife and three daughters.

Janet Nancy James

Janet is a Christian Mystic with a keen interest in and great respect for Pagan spiritual paths who has long been enthralled by the idea of Unicorns. She is an avid reader and enjoys a good debate, as much as she enjoys a good cuppa tea. After graduating from Oxford she travelled extensively before settling down back in England. She works as a transpersonal therapist.

John Canard

Having misspent most of his youth in the Cambridgeshire fens, John met the woman of his dreams, who he still believes to be only part-human and moved with her to Somerset (UK) to live the wild life. They live on a smallholding where John spends his time tending a menagerie of animals and growing organic vegetables. He is the author *of Defences of the Witches' Craft* and is working on a number of other projects on the subjects of Traditional Witchcraft and Folk Magick. To contact John email *jcherbalist@gmail.com*

Kim Huggens

Kim is a postgraduate student at Cardiff University, studying magic in the Late Antique period and in particular its influences from ancient Mesopotamia and Egypt. She is a keen Tarot enthusiast, and the co-creator of *"Sol Invictus: The God Tarot"*, published by Schiffer Books in 2007. She is currently working on *"Pistis Sophia: The Goddess Tarot"* as a companion deck with the same artist. In her spare time, Kim edits an online Pagan magazine for Cardiff University Pagan Society, writes articles, studies world mythology, and plays Dungeon and Dragons.

Magin

When she was younger Magin practiced solitary magick for about a decade, with a focus on runic divination, spellwork and witchcraft. A few years ago she also became a Wiccan, working in a coven in London. She continues being a keen student of runecraft and the Northern Tradition, expanding on her knowledge and experience whenever she gets the opportunity. She also has a growing interest in ceremonial magick and the Qabalah. Magin enjoys the creative and practical aspects of her Craft the most, and as such can often be found painting, sewing and cooking.

Marc Potts

Marc Potts is an English artist and author living and working in the beautiful and mystical Devon landscape. Marc's inspiration comes from folklore, mythology, a nature-based spirituality and a connection with the land itself. The subjects of his art are the nature-spirits, the elemental beings, the goddesses and the gods, often with more than a passing nod to the macabre and the bizarre. His art has received wide acclaim in both pagan and fantasy art circles and he has produced numerous covers for pagan and non-pagan publications, both books and magazines. Pursuing his interest in folklore, Marc has written *'The Mythology of the Mermaid and her Kin'* for Capall Bann publishing, and is currently working on an illustrated follow-up project, entitled *'Goblins'*. Marc is also working on a book project of his art, based around tree-spirits and tree-lore with a working title of *The Wyldwood*, as well as a number of illustrated short stories. Marc's art can be seen at his website *www.marcpotts.com* and *www.duirwaighgallery.com* He is available for commissions and illustration work and can be contacted by email via his website.

Nic Phillips

Nic Phillips is a Cardiff University graduate in History and Archaeology and co-author/artist of *'Sol Invictus: The God Tarot'*. He currently lives in the city centre with his partner and runs a bar by night; and in his spare time works on his art, including a follow up deck to Sol Invictus with Kim Huggens. He classes himself as primarily Pagan, with an interest in all world religions and mythology.

Nina Falaise

Nina Falaise is an artist and teacher of sacred dance. She presents dance as an alternative way to psycho-spiritual development and to liberating creativity on all levels. Nina has worked with experienced teachers of the Western Mystery Tradition since the 80's, such as Naomi Ozaniec, Marian Green, and Tony Willis. Of sacred dance Nina says, *"As the dancer moves, vibrating to the sounds of music, she creates a visual image of the unseen. Her body is the poetic voice of the unspoken"* For those who are interested in the arts and sacred dance, please contact:- *leonina.cooper@btinternet.com*

Peter J. Jaynes

Peter is passionate about the mystery traditions of ancient Europe, with a particular emphasis on the history and mythologies of the British Isles. He is a Wiccan High Priest who, with his wife, has been facilitating an initiatory Coven since the 1970's tracing their lineage back to Gerald Gardner. His work with the Horned God has taken him to many unexpected places over the years, this being the latest avenue on a labyrinth journey of possibilities.

Phil Lightwood-Jones

Phil is a part-time Egyptology student studying in Cardiff University and has attained several qualifications in the subject including a *Diploma of Higher Education in Egyptology*. He is interested in all aspects of Egyptian history with a special passion for the early periods, the religion and Gods and the ideas and the concept of Ma'at (which he defines as Universal Rightness). He is also fascinated by British Folklore and British medieval history.

Rhys Chisnall

Rhys is a member of a long established rural country coven in the north of Suffolk. He has been interested in and practicing Witchcraft for 19 years and has been fortunate enough to have been initiated into both the Gardnerian Craft which he has a great deal of respect for, and the coven he is now in with which he originally trained. Rhys has been drafted by the people who trained him, into running a pre-initiation out of coven training group for people who are seeking entry into initiatory Witchcraft.

Sorita d'Este

Author and esoteric researcher Sorita d'Este describes herself as a student of life's little mysteries. She is passionate about the western traditions of magick and mysticism, her interests and work span a wide range of subjects including the Celtic, Greek and Egyptian traditions, medieval and renaissance grimoires and palmistry. Her published works include titles such as *Practical Planetary Magick*; *Wicca Magickal Beginnings*; *The Guises of the Morrigan* and *The Isles of the Many Gods* which she co-wrote with her husband David Rankine. Sorita has lectured extensively on folklore, mythology and magick; and is the co-founder of the StarStone Network. She lives in Monmouthshire with her husband, David Rankine and their son. To find out more about her work, writings, courses and workshops see *www.avalonia.co.uk* and *www.sorita.co.uk*

Stephen Blake

Stephen Blake is a modern day philosopher, a Wiccan initiate and the possessor of a very inquiring mind eternally in search of arcane knowledge. He works in science doing things with asthma medicine and lasers, which is much less interesting than it sounds. He likes cats, sugary food, trance states, and unnecessarily complicated systems of divination. Stephen lives in London.

Thea Faye

Thea Faye is an initiate of the Mysteries and author of *Wizardry for the Uninitiated*, as well as a contributor to Scarlet Imprint's *Howlings*, other anthologies, not to mention various magazines, including *White Dragon*. Her interests currently include Wicca, Witchcraft, evocation, divination, amongst other things, but the more she studies, the more she discovers new and exciting things to learn about. A full time mother to three children, she is married to a notoriously Grumpy Badger and together, life has been one non-stop adventure since they met.

Zachary Yardley

Having read both history and science at some of the worlds most famous academic institutes, Zachary embarked on an adventure which would take him around the world a dozen or more times. He has walked on the Great Wall of China, alongside the Berlin Wall and the length of Hadrian's Wall, he has been to the pyramids in Egypt and South America, but prefers the manmade mound of Silbury Hill, Avebury. He decided a few years ago to settle down to a more predictable pace of life teaching history at a London college, which he says is a good excuse to visit the many wonderful museums and galleries London has to offer.

Zagreus

Zagreus is a team leader for the marketing department of a large corporation and wishes he wasn't. He spends his spare time wandering through museums and travelling to places with bovine connections whenever possible. He is friendly unless you approach him wearing a red shirt, when he says all bets are off.

Cornucopia:

Myth & History

THE WITCH GOD CERNUNNOS
BY SORITA D'ESTE

Primal urge of nature's power, horned god of the animals, bestower of wealth and fertility, Cernunnos is the deity who is probably cited as being *the* Horned God of witchcraft more often than any other. His name can be found in most books written on the subject of modern paganism and western initiatory Witchcraft traditions such as that of Wicca. As a Celtic god he first emerges in what is modern day France, from where his worship then seems to spread to other European countries including modern day Germany, Italy and Rumania.

The first piece of evidence for Cernunnos is the altar carving found in Notre Dame in Paris in 1710 CE which reads *'ERNUNNO'*, with the first and last letters lost through erosion. This carving from 17CE does not seem to show an antlered god, as Cernunnos is popularly perceived today, but rather a god with shorter horns. There has been speculation that the horns seen on this image are in fact those of a bull, rather than those of a stag.

It is generally accepted that the name Cernunnos simply means *'Horned One'*, but this was not always the case, as seen in Antoine Banier's *The Mythology and Fables of the Ancients* (1739). In this famous work, Banier gave the meaning of 'Horned Spear', thereby suggesting a more aggressive or maybe even bellicose nature.

Cernunnos is now generally believed to be derived from the proto-Indo-European root *krno-. This is the same word that gave rise to the Gallic *cernon*, the Welsh *carn*, the Latin *cornu* and the Germanic *hurnaz*, all of which mean *horn*. The Latin *cornu* also gave rise to words such as cornucopia (the horn of plenty) and coronet (a small crown). This latter is particularly interesting, as it indicates the position of horns at the crown, and also links the horns to royalty, reminding us of the old adage that "*the king and the land are one*". From the same original word comes the Greek word *keraunos*, meaning *thunderbolt*, further hinting at a connection to the power of the stormy sky.

In recent decades inscriptions and carvings found around Europe have shown that the Paris altar was not, as previously thought, an isolated depiction of this deity. In fact evidence for this God seems to, in actuality, be rather widespread. Cernunnos was mentioned in an inscription which was uncovered at Polenza in northern Italy, and what seems to be a depiction of a Horned God fitting his description was found at nearby Val Camonica. Variations of his name have been found at Verespatak, Rumania, where he is referred to as 'Cernenus', and as 'Deo Cernunico' at Seinsel-Rëlent in Germany. A Greek inscription which was found near Montagnac, France, is dedicated to 'Karnonos'. Of course the variations in the way the name is written are inevitable and commonplace in areas where the Romans recorded the names of local deities. This was especially true of the names of Celtic deities due to the fact that Celtic culture was oral with no written language.

However, when considering that the name and its variants mean Horned One, and looking at the diversity in images, is it perhaps more likely that Cernunnos was a title, and that as such it might have been used to refer to any horned god? Using a title for a deity name was a common practice as can be seen by looking at the names of other well known Celtic deities. For example: Morrigán (*'Great Queen'*), Daghda (*'Good God'*), Epona (*'Divine Horse'*) and Ialonus (*'God of the Glade'*). It might also be that it was a term used for a class of spiritual beings, for example the Matres (*'Mothers'*) and Genii Cucullati (*'Hooded Ones'*).

Whilst some characteristics are thus common for the type of deity represented by the title, this would also explain variations. Although there is some debate as to the nature of the horns on the Notre Dame Cernunnos, which seem more like bull horns, the other images, some of which are centuries older, clearly show him as a stag-horned god. The Val Camonica image dates to around the fourth century BCE, and shows antlers. However if this were a title, then the horned one could have antlers, bull horns or any other sort of horns depending on the localised view.

The image of the horned figure on the Gundestrup Cauldron is the best known image attributed to Cernunnos, and also shows him with antlers. This silver cauldron dates to between fourth to first century BCE and was found in Denmark. It has been shown how this figure depicted on the cauldron is probably derived from the deity Pashupati (*'Lord of the Beasts'*) or proto-Shiva. Pashupati was the main god of the Harappan culture of around 3000 BCE from the Indus Valley, and by this point he already had a huge amount in common with Cernunnos. This point is reinforced by Alain Daniélou in his work *Gods of Love and Ecstasy*, where he points out that *"All the symbols associated with the cult of Shiva – the erect phallus, the horned god, the bull, the snake, the ram, the Lady of the Mountain – are found in this cultural and agricultural complex which, starting from 6000 BC, spread westward to Europe and Africa and eastward to southern Asia."*

Moving to Rumania and the name Cernenus found there, we should also note that there has been evidence found there dating back to the period 5000-3000 BCE of a bull-horned god, also suggesting the existence of an earlier local god who assumed this name. Considering my suggestion that the name is a title, then it is possible that it was simply applied to any image of a horned male deity which fitted the local god, even though the image's origins may have been distant.

On the Gundestrup Cauldron there is also a wolf near the 'Cernunnos' figure, which is not an isolated occurrence amongst images attributed to this god, and so we may consider the wolf as another sacred animal associated with him, as suggested by researchers such as Anne Ross and Miranda Green. As a very effective hunter this would make sense. The Meigle slab in Perthshire, Scotland, which shows a Cernunnos-type figure, also has a wolf flanking it.

Another interesting feature of the Val Camonica image and some of the others, like the classic Gundestrup Cauldron image, is that he is not portrayed as being phallic. The Val Camonica image shows instead the worshipper being noticeably phallic. Again this fits if more than one deity is being depicted, with some gods being associated with fertility and others not.

Cernunnos is clearly associated with animals, as shown in the images of him (or them). He is usually shown bearing a torc and a ram-horned serpent, a symbol of chthonic wisdom and transformation, and sometimes is surrounded by other animals. In fact these particular symbols can be seen as the cult objects which positively identify an image as being a Cernunnos image. He is also known as *"the Lord of All Wild Things"*, a title which clearly demonstrates his role as an animal god.

As well as being linked to animals and thus nature, the occurrence of coins or bags of coins in images of Cernunnos, such as may be next to the god's head in the relief found at Cirencester, and in a stela found at Reims in France, point to a wealth connection as well. This association with wealth would explain why Julius Caesar chose to associate him with Dis Pater ('*the Wealthy Father*') rather than the more common Roman association of Cernunnos with Mercury. We may also note that wealth icons also indicate a fertility connection for the deity but in a different way to the ithyphallic images.

The Reims stela is interesting as it shows a horned god emptying a purse full of coins, with a bull and a stag standing below, showing both types of horned animal with him. This wealth association is also made in a relief found in Luxembourg which shows a stag vomiting money, clearly here the stag represents the horned god. At this point we should recall how the Celts avoided anthropomorphosising their gods until their exposure to the Greeks and Romans and subsequent servitude, as seen by the amusement of the Celtic leader Brennus at the Greek statues and images when they overran the Greek shrine at Delphi in 279 BCE.

Thus we must consider that some depictions of horned animals such as bulls, stags and horned serpents may in fact be representations of gods, specifically horned gods who are of the Cernunnos type. Likewise there are many unnamed figures and horned heads to be found in Britain and Europe, nearly all of which are bull-horned. We can only speculate whether any of these were a Cernunnos or specific local gods with their own names and functions.

The Romans linked Cernunnos with Mercury when they encountered him in Gaul, although as already mentioned Julius Caesar suggested a different connection, to Dis Pater, as he perceived him to be the main god of the Celts. This in itself suggests a widespread worship rather than a single local deity.

Cernunnos may have had other less considered attributes as well. The carving in Notre Dame formed part of what is known as the Boatman's Pillar due to the nautical themes on it. This has led to the suggestion that Cernunnos could also be associated with maritime themes, and certainly a relief found in Bordeaux shows a horned god holding an anchor in his left hand. The sea brings to mind trade, which also hints at the god Mercury, whose name may mean 'merchant'.

An interesting demonstration of the connection between Cernunnos and Mercury is found in a relief in York, which shows Mercury standing behind an altar. He bears the caduceus in his left hand and a large purse in the right hand. To his left stands a stag and to his right a cock. The inclusion of the stag, which was never iconically linked to Mercury by the Romans, suggests this is a conflation of the two deities. A bronze figure from St Albans showed Mercury, again with caduceus and moneybag, wearing a torc and accompanied by a ram and cock, again accompanied by a horned beast (hinting at the 'horned one'), and the ram being indicative of the ram-headed serpent. This is a much more logical conflation than might originally be considered. The ancient Greek god Hermes was largely assumed into the Roman Mercury, and his symbolic connections to Cernunnos are clearly apparent.

In addition to the dozens of carved gems of Mercury dating to the first to third century CE found in Britain, showing him bearing the caduceus and purse, there were also some found depicting a herm. A herm is a pile of stones, which were used as a boundary marker, and are connected to Hermes, the term being derived from his name. The herm was also a phallic depiction, often with the head of the god on top. As the shepherd god, and cow thief, along with his association with wealth, it is easy to see how Hermes, through his assimilation into Mercury, should be equated to

Cernunnos, the horned one who embodied wealth, fertility and nature.

When we look at the attributes that can be concretely associated with Cernunnos, it is interesting to see what is not there. Cernunnos has become incorporated into modern Wicca as the encompassing name for the Horned God as the male principle. However many of the functions he now bears are not seen in the ancient imagery, or at best are hinted at and have been brought to the fore. This could be seen as an expression of roles more appropriate to the times, and is not necessarily a bad thing. Thus it seems likely that the role of underworld god was not one seen in depictions, although the chthonic nature of the ram-horned serpent could be seen as suggesting he had chthonic connections, as could the wealth association.

As a solar god, the only image which would fit is the Mercury-like image of the god holding a wheel which is also held by a larger non-horned figure on the Gundestrup Cauldron. The wheel has eight asymmetric spokes on the half that is visible, indicating the total would be far greater, and is different from the usual six spokes seen born by the Wheel God in Celtic art. The wheel has been linked to the Gallic Celtic god Taranis ('thunder') and the Roman god Jupiter as a solar symbol, and so this could provide a tentative link for the solar connection.

From the hints in the stories, it seems likely that Cernunnos also went underground into the Christian church to survive the new religion. The early pope Cornelius, a close friend of Saint Cyprian, was pope from 251-253 CE before being forced out of office. He was canonised to Saint Cornelius, his name meaning horn, and was depicted with his iconic attribute of a bull horn. Cornelius is the patron saint of farmers and cattle, so he is a horned saint of horned beasts! One story tells how the stones at Carnac (note the name again associated with horn) were actually a pagan army chasing

Cornelius, who turned them to stone. The Christian gloss given to earlier pagan images strongly suggest that he was in fact Cernunnos made respectable!

What is clear is that Cernunnos, whether he was a specific god or whether the name was a title for a range of gods, has become far more widely worshipped and gained far more attributes than he had two thousand years ago. Now he is worshipped worldwide as the divine male principle, and gods whose worship may have eclipsed his are now in his shadow. The Horned One has made the transition to the modern age, whilst still retaining the original characteristics that made him so popular. Truly we can see through his success that Cernunnos bears the horns of power.

Bibliography

Banier, Antoine; *The Mythology and Fables of the Ancients*; 1739; A Millar; London

Brown, Norman O.; *Hermes the Thief*; 1990; Lindisfarne Press; Massachusetts

Daniélou, Alain; *Gods of Love and Ecstasy: The Traditions of Shiva and Dionysus*; 1992; Inner Traditions International; Vermont

Davidson, Hilda Ellis; *The Lost Beliefs of Northern Europe*; 1999; Barnes & Noble; New York

Gimbutas, Marija; *Anza ca 6500-5000 BC: A Cultural Yardstick for the Study of Neolithic Southeast Europe*; in *Journal of Field Archaeology Vol 1.1*; 1974; Boston University

Henig, Martin; *A Corpus of Roman Engraved Gemstones from British Sites* (2 vols); 1974; BAR; Oxford

Olmsted, G.S.; *The Gundestrup Cauldron*; 1979; in *Collection Latomus 162*; Brussels

Rankine, David; & d'Este, Sorita; *The Isles of the Many Gods*; 2007; Avalonia; London

Ross, Anne; *Pagan Celtic Britain*; 1967; Routledge & Kegan Paul Ltd; London

HERNE: THE ROYAL HUNTER
BY HORTUS ST MICHAEL

The tragedy of Herne played out in the reign of Richard II, twenty-three years full of strife, ruled over by a young King who some say was badly advised. Richard II came to the throne in 1377 when he was ten years old, and reigned until he died in 1400, his throne usurped and he a prisoner.

King Richard loved to hunt, and one of the best places to hunt was the royal estate around Windsor Castle. Herne was one of the huntsmen employed by the King, who loved his job and the forest he plied his craft in. Few indeed could be considered as skilled as Herne; he was a superlative huntsman who knew every track in the wood, the ways of every creature, and every trick of the hunt. When the King was at Windsor Castle for the hunt, Herne would accompany him almost every day, guiding his King to the best game.

Early one morning the royal hounds caught the rarest of scents, the elusive white stag, called by some the messenger of the spirits. The King and his party gave chase, the hounds drawing close and the horses with their riders gaining on the noble stag. Ahead flashes of white showed him leaping through the trees and undergrowth, seeking to escape the ever-tightening net of hounds and hunters. Arrows flew, the stag stumbled, its blood flowing from the wounds it took. Mighty still it bounded on, through the dense undergrowth and into a clearing where it stopped. The trees were tightly packed together; there was no way out save back past the hunters.

The mighty white stag, dripping red blood onto the forest floor, turned to face its pursuers, pawing the ground and raising its many tines in defiant challenge. The master of the hounds ordered his men to leash the dogs and hold them back. Everyone kept their distance, forming a semi-circle around the stag preventing it from escaping. The King rode forward, unsheathing his knife to make the kill, for only he could make the kill with such a noble beast. Before Richard had a chance to dismount, the stag burst into action, springing at the King, and disembowelling his horse with his mighty antlers. As the King fell to the ground Herne leapt forward, bravely pushing the King aside and taking the full brunt of the stag's rage in his place. Pierced by the antlers he fell, his own knife ripping the life out of the stag in return as he cut its throat. The white stag lay dead, with Herne dying next to it on the blood-soaked forest floor. Whether he was just a loyal man, or the willing sacrifice to protect the King from some vengeance of the spirits, Herne had saved his monarch and paid the price.

As Herne lay bleeding the King called for his physician, but he was back at the castle. No-one could help and the King watched on helpless as Herne lay dying. Then, as if from nowhere, a man on a black horse appeared from behind a large beech tree. Philip Urswick, for such he called himself, introduced himself to the King and offered his services. Some cried he must be a poacher, out after the stag himself, but others recognised him and told the King of his deeds. For Urswick was a wizard, who dwelled nearby on Bagshot Heath, though being black clad on a black horse there were some who claimed he was the devil himself. Knowing that Urswick was the only chance Herne had, the King gave his permission for him to tend Herne's wounds.

Urswick studied Herne's wounds and muttered a charm too softly for any to make out. He turned to two of the huntsmen and instructed them to remove the antlers from the dead stag to be fixed to Herne's head. The bewildered huntsmen looked at their King, who nodded his agreement, willing to try anything. The bloody antlers were tied to Herne's head and he was carried on a litter through the forest to Urswick's hut on Bagshot Heath. Still as a corpse Herne lay for the whole journey, giving no sign that he was still alive. After a month of treatment by Urswick, drinking strange potions and covered with lotions, the antlers came off and Herne returned to the Castle in good health. King Richard was so delighted to see his young rescuer in good health he rewarded him with a golden chain, a silver hunting horn and a bag of gold, and bade him move into the royal apartments in Windsor Castle. Herne became the royal favourite, accompanying the King everywhere.

The King's favour was in great demand, and many jealous gazes and whispers were to be found in the court at Herne's rapid rise to royal confidant. Jealous huntsmen started a story that Herne had learned the magickal arts from Urswick, and was now a wizard himself who had bewitched the King. When the King heard this he laughed and dismissed the idea, ending the gossip. King Richard was no fool and had already had Philip Urswick thoroughly investigated after his forest encounter. He was satisfied that Urswick was a good man who used his skills benevolently, and not for malice.

Their first attempt having failed so completely, the huntsmen came up with another plan. They planted three fresh deer skins in his quarters, prior to starting a rumour that he was poaching. As they waked away from his room the conspirators bumped into

Herne. Oblivious to the treachery of his supposed friends, Herne gave them a purse of money and asked them to deliver it to Urswick as a token of his appreciation.

Filled with the poison of jealousy the huntsmen saw an even better way to bring Herne down. Pocketing the money, they made their way to Urswick's hut to spread their lies. They told Urswick that both Herne and the King had forgotten them. The King had given many gifts to Herne but ignored all of Urswick's hard work. Not only this but Herne claimed that Urswick had kept him prisoner and only pretended to heal him, when he had in fact only fainted after being attacked by the stag and had not been nearly as injured as it had appeared.

As is often the case, the liars made their stories sound so plausible that even a wizard such as Urswick believed them, or so it seemed. Furious, Urswick sought a way to have his revenge on the ungrateful Herne. Perhaps he should remove Herne's hunting skills, suggested the betrayers. Urswick agreed and worked his magick, but only on condition that the huntsmen would agree to whatever he next asked them. Flushed with their own success and not considering the implications of the wizard's request, the huntsmen agreed. For several days Herne, usually the most skilled tracker, could not find a single piece of game for his King to hunt. It was at this point, when Herne's skill had deserted him, that the hidden hides were conveniently found in his quarters. A furious Richard jumped to the conclusion the jealous huntsmen had set for him, assuming that Herne had abused his position and was poaching at night, and that he was too tired to find game for his King by day. In a fit of rage King Richard dismissed Herne from the court.

Betrayed and publicly humiliated, his skills magickally stripped from him, Herne rode off into the forest distraught. The next morning a pedlar found Herne's body hanging from an oak tree. He had killed himself, unable to live with the disgrace that had been brought upon him. The huntsmen gloated and sought the favour they felt Herne had denied them. But nothing went right for the treacherous men. They started to lose their hunting skill, and they were left behind during hunts. Unable to cope, the huntsmen went to see Urswick to seek his aid.

Urswick told the huntsmen that they would have to appeal to Herne's ghost for mercy, at the very oak where he had killed himself. The nervous huntsmen followed him to the oak, where Urswick called for Herne's ghost to appear, which he did, complete with antlers. Herne told the huntsmen they would have to return the next night at midnight to the same spot, bringing all the royals hounds and horses. The terrified huntsmen, desperate to placate the angry ghost, agreed.

Each night following Herne led the huntsmen through the forest, catching every deer and piece of game until there was nothing there for the King to catch during the day. The furious King summoned his huntsmen demanding an explanation, and they confessed the whole story. Full of remorse, King Richard took a walk into the forest to consider what he had been told.

As he wandered through the trees a storm appeared out of nowhere. As the King started heading for shelter a nearby oak was blasted by lightning. Through the smoke King Richard saw an antlered figure, and realised this was the oak which Herne had hung himself from. Herne approached the King and demanded justice. Kill the huntsmen as he had died, said Herne, and the forest would be returned to the King.

The King had the huntsmen hung from Herne's oak, and all the deer returned to the forest. Herne himself was not seen again until the day of King Richard II's death. Since then he has returned every winter with his followers, the Wild Hunt as they are known, claiming souls for his eternal hunt. And he is a terrifying sight by all accounts, riding a fiery black steed, and is outlined with a blue fiery light. A horned owl sits on one shoulder and he rattles the gold chain given to him by King Richard. Herne is also said to appear when the sovereign of Britain is near to death, or is unjust, or when the nation is in danger.

'Herne, The Hunter in Windsor Great Park',

HERO LORD OF ANNWFN

BY GARETH GERRARD

Round-hoofed is my horse, the torment of battle,
Fairy am I called, Gwynn the son of Nudd,
The lover of Creiddylad, the daughter of Lludd.[1]

Although not technically a Horned God, the Cymric underworld deity Gwynn ap Nudd certainly fits the profile. Lord of the Otherworld, having dominion over demonic forces, king of the Faery and leader of the Wild Hunt, he is attributed a number of mythic archetypes: prodigious warrior and Arthurian hero, abductor of the spring maiden and participator in a cyclical battle over her possession, psychopomp and hunter of souls, attended by a pack of ferocious unearthly hounds. From obscure beginnings, his name has resonated down the ages and gained a firm foot-hold in the imagination of poets, story tellers and practitioners of modern paganism alike.

I first heard his name at Samhain at an open ritual hosted by a group in my home town of Cardiff many years ago. It was my inaugural Sabbat experience, and as such, most of what occurred

---

[1] The Black Book Of Carmarthen, poem 33

was new and unfamiliar, but I can remember my curiosity being piqued by the name Gwynn ap Nudd during the invocation of the God. I had never to my knowledge heard the name before, but for some reason it lodged in my head like a seed patiently awaiting more favourable conditions before commencing growth.

In common with many of the Welsh deities found in the extant texts, it is unlikely that pre-Christian Britons ever worshipped him as a god in his own right. But it is certain that those ancient Cymric poets and safe-keepers of the oral tradition drew inspiration from mythic cycles never committed to the written word, and that the spirit alluded to in the manuscripts represents a powerful and enduring archetype.

Paradoxically for a deity who has become associated with an underworld archetype, the theonym Gwyn translates as *'white'*, but with an allusion to *'fair'*, *'blessed'*, *'bright'* or even *'Holy'*. Nudd, his father, was another battle god cognate with the Celtic god Nodens, to whom a temple complex is located at Lydney Park overlooking the Severn Estuary. Gwynn ap Nudd is recognized as the Cymric equivalent of the Irish Fionn mac Cumhaill.

Gwynn ap Nudd appears in the medieval Welsh heroic prose Culhwch and Olwen, one of the so called *Native Tales* from *The Mabinogion*.[2] *The Mabinogion*, originally compiled and translated into English between 1838 and 1849 by Lady Charlotte Guest, consists of three thematically distinct and broadly contiguous sections: the *Four Branches of The Mabinogi*, the five *Native Tales*, and the *Three Romances*. The main sources for the translation were two extant Welsh codices, *Llyfr Gwyn Rhydderch* (*White Book of Rhydderch*) and *Llyfr Coch Hergest* (*Red Book of Hergest*) both dating from the mid to late thirteenth century, their names deriving from the colour of their binding, along with a few other fragmentary manuscripts. It is

---

[2] Translated by Jeffrey Gantz, Penguin Edition, 1976,

likely that the original written form of the tales, drawing heavily from older oral tradition, predate these collections by maybe anything up to a couple of centuries.[3]

Gwynn is described in one tale in the *Mabinogion, Culhwch and Olwen*, as being, *'in whom God has set the spirit of the demons of Annwfn, lest this world be destroyed,'* indicating that he has at least some dominion over the Otherworld, Annwfn. We can also infer that he is an agent of balance and control, charged with ensuring that the mortal plane is not unduly influenced by the underworld realm of Annwfn. In later tales, he also identified as King of the *Tylwyth Teg* (*'Fair-Folk'* or faery), and becomes associated with the *Cŵn Annwfn* (Otherworld hunting dogs with shining white bodies and blood red ears and eyes), and the Wild Hunt of pan-European legend.

Although Annwfn (lit, *in-world*) is cognate as the Cymric Hades, it was far from being a place of banishment, punishment or suffering; pejorative qualities peculiar to Christian interpretation. Indeed, it was considered a fair realm replete with fountains of sweet flowing wine; in modern Brittany, Annaon translates as Paradise, and the phrase, *'mont da Annaon'* is a euphemism for death.[4] The *Mabinogion* provides us with no less than four rulers of Annwfn: Arawn, Hafgan, Pwyll and Gwynn. The First Branch, *Pwyll, Prince of Dyfed*, identifies Arawn and Hafgan as being co-rulers in contention for supremacy, a conflict in which Arawn emerges victorious due to the help of Pwyll, who rules Annwfn in his stead for a year and dispatches Hafgan with a single blow. Arawn is then proclaimed sole ruler of Annwfn and Pwyll receives the epithet Pwyll pen Annwfn (Pwyll, head of Annwfn).

Since both Arawn and Gwynn ap Nudd are associated with rulership of Annwfn, the Cŵn Annwfn, and the Wild Hunt, it

---

[3] James MacKillop, Dictionary of Celtic Mythology, Oxford 1998
[4] The Mabinogion, pp228, translated by Sioned Davies, Oxford 2007

becomes difficult to sufficiently differentiate them as not being synonymous. However, there is no obvious etymological correlation between the two theonyms (Arawn has been reported as being derived from the Proto-Celtic meaning free-thinking masculine spirit). Another idea is that Arawn may be more a title than an actual name, which would certainly strengthen the argument of a synonymous association between the two. This becomes more pertinent in modern usage, especially when considering the syncretic fusion of both ancient Gaulish gods (Cernunnos) and folkloric figures (Herne the Hunter) into the Horned God egregore.

Culhwch and Olwen is possibly the earliest Arthurian tale, predating both Geoffrey of Monmouth and Chrétien de Troyes. Gwynn's role in the story is only a minor one, almost a cameo, but the few pertinent stanzas provide us with a wealth of insight. King Arthur agrees to help young Culhwch win the hand of the maiden Olwen from her father, the giant Ysbaddaden. And to this end Arthur assembles a host of heroes from the length and breadth of Briton, Gwynn being named among them. However, before Arthur can recruit Gwynn, he has to resolve a conflict between him and Gwythyr fab Greidawl over the abduction of the maiden, Creiddylad. Gwythyr fab Greidawl translates as 'Victor, son of Scorcher', denoting a summer-solar association.

Creiddylad, daughter of Lludd Llaw Ereint (Silver-Hand; Lludd interestingly, is a cognate of Nudd, Gwynn's father) and '*the most majestic maiden there ever was in the three Islands of Britain*'[5] had promised herself to Gwythyr. However, before they can consummate their union, she is taken by force by Gwyn ap Nudd, precipitating a battle between him and a host raised by Gwythyr, in which Gwynn is victorious. Gwynn then takes a number of nobles

---

[5] *Ibid, pp189*

as hostages and even causes one to lose his sanity by forcing him to eat his slain father's heart! Arthur, upon hearing of these occurrences, travels *'into the North'* and brokers peace between the factions, releasing the hostages and causing Gwynn and Gwythyr to resolve their quarrel by playing out a familiar mythic motif. They are to engage in single combat every *Calan Mai* (May Day) until Doomsday, whilst Creiddylad remains with her father, and the victor on Doomsday will have her hand.

Here we see a familiar seasonal leitmotif of solar and chthonic deity, representing the light and dark halves of the year (cf Oak King and Holly King) struggling for determination over the fate of the land's fecundity. Creiddylad, the embodiment of fertile potential, becomes the Cymric Persephone, whose cyclical association with the Underworld signals the end of the period of growth and abundance precipitated by the onset of winter.

In the *Black Book of Carmarthen*, the earliest of the extant Welsh texts, Gwynn ap Nudd is portrayed as the victorious warrior, magnanimous at the parley, and during the course of the conversation with Gwyddno, he reveals himself to be a supranatural entity, cognate with the god of death and battle, and a psychopomp − *'I am the escort of the grave.'*[6] The poem is long and alliterative, making many references to ravens crying over the battle, a motif familiar in both Irish (The Morrigán) and Norse (Odin) mythic poetry. The link with Odin, as both a god of death and of inspiration and poetry, is given in a 14th Century Latin text, which amounts as an invocation to Gwynn ap Nudd by Welsh soothsayers, *"to the king of Spirits and to his consort, Gwyn ap Nudd, you who are yonder in the forest, for love of your mate, permit us to enter your dwelling."* This seems to suggest that the state of divine

---

[6] The Black Book of Carmarthen, poem 33

inspiration entered into by the soothsayer was associated with the realm of Gwynn and his consort, about whom nothing is written.

Another famous Welsh story from which we learn much about Gwynn ap Nudd's perceived character concerns the legendary 7th century Abbot of Glastonbury, St Collen, after whom the Welsh town of Llangollen is named. The story was translated by Lady Charlotte Guest and appended to her edition of the *Mabinogion*, but is generally omitted from later versions.[7]

After a pious and eventful life, St Collen retires from the Abbey, and such is his disgust at the ungodly ways of his fellow countrymen, he damns them and retreats into anchoritic solitude. One day he hears two people passing his cell discussing the Lord of Annwfn and King of the Tylwyth Teg, Gwynn ap Nudd. Collen immediately reprimands them and denigrates Gwynn and the Tylwyth Teg as devils, to which the men warn him not to speak such, as Gwynn will find out. Sure enough, later that day a messenger from Gwynn summons Collen to meet with Gwynn on the summit of the hill at midday to explain his slander. Collen ignores the summons and again the next day. The third day he agrees to attend, and meets with Gwynn as requested, but as a precaution he conceals a phial of holy water. There is nothing at the summit of the hill, but as he turns to leave a castle and fabulous retinue appear. Collen is taken to meet Gwynn, who is regal and courteous and takes pains to make Collen welcome, offering him food, wine and music for his pleasure. Collen rejects all offers, dismisses Gwynn's retinue as infernal and repays Gwynn's hospitality by splashing his realm with holy water. Gwynn and his realm immediately disappear, leaving Collen alone and unharmed on the hill.

---

[7] Buchedd Collen, 1536, Hafod MS 19, pp141

Here we see an unveiling of the dynamic stresses not just between the new (Christian) order and the old (pagan) ways, but maybe an underpinning of the changes happening within British Christianity as European fervour and piety begin to replace the more relaxed and inclusive Celtic Church of the medieval period. Either way, Gwynn is shown as being helpful and diplomatic, seeking a compromise with the new ways. Collen, on the other hand, comes across as narrow-minded and inflexible. The good grace of Gwynn is illustrated by the fact that he simply removes his realm at the insult of the old Abbot and leaves him alive to pursue his miserable isolated existence. But the world is left poorer and diminished in colour. That is until a more receptive and understanding time, where he and the Tylwyth Teg may once more open their realm.

Bibliography
Anon; *The Black Book Of Carmarthen*, poem 33
Davies, Sioned (trans); *The Mabinogion*; 2007; Oxford
Gantz, Jeffrey (trans); *The Mabinogion*; 1976; Penguin Edition
MacKillop, James; *Dictionary of Celtic Mythology*; 1998; Oxford

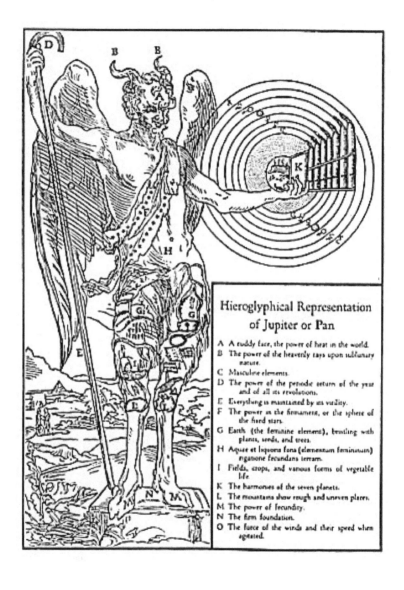

Hieroglyphical Representation of Jupiter or Pan

A   A ruddy face, the power of heat in the world.
B   The power of the heavenly rays upon sublunary nature.
C   Masculine elements.
D   The power of the periodic return of the year and of all its revolutions.
E   Everything is maintained by its virility.
F   The power in the firmament, or the sphere of the fixed stars.
G   Earth (the feminine element), bristling with plants, seeds, and trees.
H   Aquae et liquoris fons (elementum femininum) riganone fecundans terram.
I   Fields, crops, and various forms of vegetable life.
K   The harmonies of the seven planets.
L   The mountains show rough and uneven places.
M   The power of fecundity.
N   The firm foundation.
O   The force of the winds and their speed when agitated.

PAN: THE HIDDEN ALL

BY DAVID RANKINE

Wild God, who lifted me from earth,
Who taught me freedom, wisdom, mirth,
Immortalized my body's worth.

From: A Note From the Pipes, Leonora Speyer

Priapic gods are often clichéd or trivialized due to the emphasis on their obvious phallicism. For me this has seemed especially true of Pan. However phallicism does not always simply equate to sexuality, or at least conventional sexuality. Pan was said to have invented masturbation (as mentioned by a number of classical writers, including Catullus, Dio Chryostomus and Ovid), which together with tales of his attempts at molesting nymphs and his passion for goats resulted in his categorization by early psychologists as representing the darker side of sexuality.

Additionally Pan is not entirely heterosexual, rather he is a bisexual god. This is shown by the story of Pan and the shepherd Daphnis, and best depicted on the famous statue of Pan sitting teaching Daphnis to play the pan-pipes, with one arm around him. A depiction on a vase showed a very phallic Pan pursuing a goatherd, watched on by a very phallic Hermes (his father), showing Daphnis was not a one-off.

Of course Pan is famous for causing panic, feelings of fear caused by his presence, as he was usually not seen but felt by people travelling through the lonely wild places. So from these perspectives it is understandable that a clichéd view of Pan should have arisen. However, any coin has two sides, and there is also a positive view of Pan, both in the ancient world and in the modern world. One quality of Pan which is prominent in both views of the horned god is that Pan was both the god of the flock, protecting animals, and at the same time the god of the hunt, with his pack of hunting dogs. And then there was the music. The haunting and lonely beauty of the pan-pipes is surely one of the most poignant sounds you can hear, and Pan invented it! Playing with pipes was clearly something Pan was very good at.

When Hermes found the baby Pan, who had been abandoned by his nurse in fear at his unusual appearance, he took him to Olympus. There Pan's boisterous behaviour delighted the gods, who named him Pan (*'All'*) as he amused them all. So Pan was popular not only in rustic circles, called on by shepherds to protect their flocks, and by hunters for success, but also amongst the gods themselves. Of course Pan is an inspirational god, as can be seen in some of the poems and fiction written by writers such as Percy Bysshe Shelley (*Hymn of Pan*), Elizabeth Barrett Browning (*A Musical Instrument*), Aleister Crowley (*Hymn to Pan*) and Arthur Machen (*The Great God Pan*). Early writers too picked up on Pan, like John Fletcher in the late sixteenth century with his *Hymn to Pan*. Indeed once you start looking, it is amazing how Pan turns up all over the place. You can't keep a good god down, he is mentioned in the writings of Oscar Wilde, John Keats, William Wordsworth, Algernon Swinburne, and the list goes on. A classic modern reference can be found in the iconic song *The Return of Pan*, by The Waterboys.

Pan was a very popular god in Victorian times, possibly because of what was perceived as his *"quaint, rustic charm"* at a time where the *"noble savage"* was being held up as a symbol of the power of primitive nature. And of course the great tour through Europe to Italy and Greece would have left indelible impressions in many young men's minds. Statues of Pan appeared in the gardens of stately homes, along with Poseidon and Aphrodite and other Greek gods. So has Pan become more popular in modern times than he was in the ancient world? It has been argued that we have a very sanitized view of Pan today, that he was a raw and uncouth rapist who was never a major god.

Well Arcadian Pan did have his temples, but it must be remembered that he was a Chthonic god rather than an Olympian god. I.e. he was worshipped with altars on the ground, not ones set into the air like a table. And many of Pan's sacred places were caves and mountains and places in nature, rather than man-made structures. After all he is a nature god, and the best way to worship him is in nature.

Pan is one of the gods particularly associated with music and dance, which is not what you might expect for such an allegedly coarse god. Pan is described by the Greek writer Pindar as *choreutan teleōtaton* (*"the most complete dancer"*). Unlike the aloof Apollo, Pan not only leads the dance as *choregos*, but also joins in with the other dancers. Pan was particularly to be found dancing with nymphs, who were famous for their grace. What is significant about Pan's dancing is that it goes beyond dancing for pleasure and into the realms of magickal transformation. Plato in his *Laws* classified dances imitating Pan's as being initiatory and purificatory. However there is an even greater power to Pan's dancing. It was believed that when Pan danced the boundaries between the worlds could be loosened, so it might become possible to escape from the underworld, for example.

Pindar's description of Pan as *"guardian of untrodden places"* emphasises his role as the wilderness god, a point also emphasised in the *Homeric Hymn to Pan*:

"He claims every snowy peak and mountain top and rocky headland. He goes here and there among the close underbrush, now drawn by the gentle streams, now he wanders among the sun-swept peaks, climbing to the highest peak that overlooks the flocks. Often he runs through the white lofty mountains, and often he, the keen-eyed god, speeds along the shoulders of the mountain slaying beasts."

Combining these qualities it becomes clear that Pan is a liminal god, who both moves through the liminal and also creates the liminal with that movement. His is entirely in keeping with his nature as the main son of Hermes, the supreme psychopomp and messenger of the Olympian gods. This convergence of qualities of Pan was emphasised in a magickal working to Pan I was involved with back in the mid 1980s in Oxford with a couple of good friends who are both very effective magicians, Jack Daw and Katon Shual. In the ritual, Pan said: *"My rites are of lust and joy and ecstasy. Let the psyche be rendered and let the universe be destroyed at the climax of your rites, that they may be reformed in love and laughter."*

PAN.

Revisiting this statement now with a far greater knowledge of Pan, with far more quality research available providing more glimpses into the ancient world, the combination of his qualities, both unknown and known, in this statement, is beautifully poetic and for me sums up Pan better than anything dry that is written about him. One of the most interesting qualities of Pan is his unpredictable nature. He is one of the gods representing the amoral and often chaotic power of nature, manifesting the dark and hidden forces. He does not fall into convenient predictable patterns. If you work with Pan to bring change into your life, he is happy to oblige, but it may manifest in very unexpected ways. This is part of his charm. Pan is not a god to call on if you like everything neatly ordered, numbered and packed in boxes.

Pan's companionship of Dionysus shows another side to his character. The ecstatic human form of Dionysus and the wild half-goat form of Pan are ideal companions, representing the spectrum from animal through human to divine. Of course we should not forget that Dionysus himself was also a bull-horned god, as seen by titles such as Horned Child, Bull-horned and Bull-browed. This is made clear by Euripides in *The Bacchantes*, where he wrote concerning his gestation in the thigh of Zeus, *"And when the Fates had fully formed the horned god, he brought him forth and crowned him with a coronal of snakes."*

A good example of Pan's ability to turn something on its head in an unexpected manner can be seen in the phrase *"Et In Arcadia Ego"* (I was in Arcadia). This phrase has been adopted by conspiracy buffs, due to its use as a title by the Renaissance artist Nicholas Poussin for two of his significantly symbolic paintings. It has been suggested that this phrase is an anagram for *"I! Tego arcana dei"* (Begone, I keep God's secrets), suggesting the tomb is that of Jesus. Were this the case, the claim that when Jesus was born a voice cried *"Pan is dead"* is by implication turned on its head by his worshippers (Arcadian shepherds) studying the tomb of the dead Christ in the paintings.

Whilst Pan is probably one of the last gods I would associate with gematria, it is interesting to look at his name and some of the other Greek words which add to the same total. Pan adds to 131 (Pi = 80; Alpha = 1; Nu = 50), as do the ancient Greek words for change (AMOIBH) and seed or origin (GONH). The spelling of Pan as Panes adds to 401, the same as time (KAIROS) and pure or perfect (KAThAROS). It is almost impossible not to note the synchronicity of appropriate meanings for the words which add to the same as his name, as they fit so well.

So although he has been demonized and trivilialised, it can be seen that the great god Pan, the liminal horned dancer of the wild places, is actually one of the most magickal of gods, initiator and bringer of change. Rumours of his death have been greatly exaggerated; Pan is alive and well and will outlive humanity.

Bibliography
Allen, Thomas W., & Sikes, E.E.; *The Homeric Hymns*; 1904; Macmillan and Co; London
Boardman, John; *The Great God Pan: The Survival of an Image (Walter Neurath Memorial Lectures)*; 1998; Thames & Hudson, London
Borgeaud, Philippe; *The Cult of Pan in Ancient Greece*; 1988; University of Chicago Press; Chicago
Daniélou, Alain; *Gods of Love and Ecstasy: The Traditions of Shiva and Dionysus*; 1992; Inner Traditions International; Vermont
Hillman, James; *Pan and the Nightmare*; 2000; Spring Publications Inc
Lonsdale, Steven H.; *Dance and Ritual Play in Greek Religion*; 1993; John Hopkins
Skinner, Marilyn B.; *Sexuality in Greek and Roman Culture*; 2005; Blackwell Publishing
Vinci, Leo; *Pan: Great God of Nature*; 1993; Neptune Press, London

Veles by Nic Phillips, from the Sol Invictus God Tarot

VELES IN SLAVIC MYTH
BY KIM HUGGENS

Due to the fact that the Slavic peoples had no written language until the 9th century, and they adopted Christianity as their official religion not long after in 988 CE, the little that can be called Slavic mythology comes to us in a heavily fragmented form. It is found only in a small number of historical accounts, folk customs, and folk songs that seem to have forgotten the old Gods almost entirely, and mention them almost in passing or as an example of superstitious nonsense. In some cases in seems that the old Slavic Gods are written about without the realisation that that is indeed what they are! Such historical accounts that have been preserved over the centuries were written after the worship of the Slavic Gods became mingled with that of the Christian God and the Saints. Many of these accounts are difficult to translate and put into context, and as such there is an ongoing debate as to their usefulness in studying Slavic myths. What seems to be the case, however, is that the growing Christian religion did not simply conquer and replace the old Slavic religion. Instead there are a number of cases of Slavic Gods becoming synonymous with Christian Saints in the minds of the *"two-faithed"*: the Slavs who saw

Christianity as an addition to their original beliefs and practices instead of a replacement. One of these sainted Gods is Veles, the God depicted surrounded by cattle and with the horns of a bull on his head.

Veles was also known as Volos, Vles, Weles, and Voloh, and for the Baltic peoples he was called Vélinas, Velnias, or Vels. The earliest mention we have of him is in the *Primary Chronicle* from the 10th century, in which an account is given where the Slavs make an oath of peace upon the name of Veles and his counterpart and opponent Perun. It was written that if the oath-swearers were to break this oath, Perun (God of thunder and war) would cause them to die in battle and Veles would make them turn *"as yellow as gold"* – the yellow skin of disease. In this account Veles is a God who blesses oaths, trades, and promises, as well as a God with a mastery over the physical body. Interestingly, Veles also seems to be a God of the common people as opposed to Perun who is a God of the Prince and his troops: in the *Chronicle*, the leader and army swear their peace oath on Perun, whilst the people swear the same oath to Veles. His status as the peoples' God is supported by *A Tale of Vladmir's Baptism*, which tells us that while he was still pagan, Vladimir I, Prince of Kiev, erected a statue of Veles which stood in the tradesman's quarter/marketplace of the city. This is in direct opposition to the several other statues of Gods (including Perun) that he had erected on the hill by the palace and royal quarters. Sadly, this statue was destroyed shortly after Vladimir was baptised a Christian.

Veles did not just have connotations with commerce and trading, however – he was primarily seen (and depicted) as a God of cattle and wild animals. He was sometimes referred to as skotjibog – *"cattle-god"*, and was also associated with the annual harvest and the fruitfulness of the earth and the animals that grazed upon it. Veles wasn't just the lord of the earth, but also the lord of under the earth or the Underworld – which the Slavs believed was a beautiful, lush place where spring was eternal and there was plenty of fresh water to drink. The souls of the dead would be expected to watch the cattle herds belonging to Veles in the Underworld.

The main myth of Veles is that of his yearly battle with Perun, the God of storm and war. Although in all versions of this myth we know that a theft instigated the battle, it is uncertain what was stolen (it is variously cattle, rainwater, a son, or a wife) and by whom: although Veles is the God of cattle he is sometimes said to steal cattle from Perun, for instance. In the myth the two Gods fought each other, and Perun threw lightning bolts at Veles who transformed into different animals and hid from his attacker. Perun finally killed him, bringing about a ritual death in which Veles' dead body poured onto the earth what he had stolen in the form of life-nourishing rainwater. This battle was said to recur every year, and can be interpreted as the Slavic explanation of the seasonal cycles, and the beginning of a rainy season. Thus, Veles became a sacrificial deity synonymous with the cyclical earth. In this sense he shares a mythological role with the Icelandic Ymir and the Indian Purusa: according to the *Eddas* the world came into being from the dead body of the frost giant Ymir (*Prose Edda, Glyfaginning 8*), and in the *Rig Veda* the Gods create the world by dismembering the cosmic giant (also viewed as the primeval male) Purusa (*Rig Veda 10.90*). Some commentators, such as Russian philologists Vyacheslav Vsevolodovich Ivanov and Vladimir Toporov, have speculated that the similarities between the myth of Veles and Perun's yearly combat and that of other sacrificial beings is due to a common Indo-European root.

Although Veles, who is often said to fight in the form of a dragon or serpent, is killed by Perun the myth does not equate with similar dragon-slaying stories in which the dragon/serpent is a force of evil and the triumphant slayer a force of good. Veles is viewed as a benevolent deity (although if he is angered he will afflict people and cattle with disease), and is often prayed to for good fortune and blessing. A harvest custom found in many Slavic nations, which continued well past the Christianization of the area, was to cut the first ear of wheat and tie it into an amulet that would protect the harvest from evil spirits. This was known as *"tying the beard of Veles."*

As the God of the dead, Veles was known to send ancestral spirits out of the Underworld and across the sea to the land of the living during the end of Winter festivals, when the veil between the two worlds was thinnest. It was believed that these spirits would find their way to their ancestral homes and celebrate the festivities with their family. As such, Veles can be viewed as a God of family ties, heritage, and knowing one's roots.

Despite his sometimes macabre and aggressive associations, Veles does not appear to have been viewed as a dark or unhappy character: instead, he is depicted as a God of musicians as well, and every year during the celebration of the return of Veles' dead from the Underworld, men would roam the town singing songs about the afterlife. They were greeted warmly by every household and given gifts – much like carol singers of later centuries! This yearly return of the beloved dead to their ancestors also does not appear to have been viewed with fear or apprehension, as we have no surviving records of any steps taken to ensure the safety of the living on this night. We can suppose that this event was instead a joyous occasion of comfort and welcome towards the souls of the departed.

With Christianity Veles did not die but instead became St. Blaise (St. Vlasy/St. Vlas), a Saint of cattle, wool-working, animals, builders, stone-cutters, and carvers. In Yarosavl the first church built over a shrine of Veles was dedicated to St. Blaise. The Acts of St. Blaise, while possibly not authentic, describe him as having a natural affinity for animals to the extent that herds and flocks would come to receive his blessing. On his feast day, February 11th, Russian peasants would drive their cattle to church and have them blessed and protected against disease through prayer. It is also possible that Veles was sainted and split into more than one Saint – St. Blaise and St. Nicholas. Eastern Slavic stories show his as St. Nicholas protecting farmers, and bequeathing unexpected wealth upon deserving people.

Veles' worship hasn't died a death even yet however, despite his Christianization and the eventual death of original Slavic paganism in the 20th century. With the advent of a modern form of Slavic paganism, a text known as *"The Book of Veles"* has come to light. This text supposedly reports events that occurred as early as the 7th century BCE and is given an authorship date of the 9th-10th century CE. It details a history of the Slavic peoples – their migration from Kazakhstan, through Syria, and finally into the Carpathian mountains, their battles against various invading tribes and peoples, and their defeat by the Normans. In the text there are several mentions of supposed Slavic deities, Veles being among them though not a prominent figure in any way. The title given to the text is not due to any special treatment of Veles but instead a reference to a particular line of the text: *"...to Veles this book we devote."*

The Book of Veles is used as a holy text by many modern Slavic Pagans, yet scholarship and commentary upon the book is skeptical. Most scholars view the book as an elaborate forgery from either the 1800's or 1940's, and certainly their arguments are damning. However, the text is an inspiration to Slavic Pagans who continue to worship Veles amongst other deities from the Slavic lands.

Bibliography

Cross, Samuel H. (ed); *Russian Primary Chronicle: Laurentian Text*; 1968; Medieval Academy of Amer

Dixon-Kennedy, Mike; *Encyclopedia of Russian and Slavic Myth and Legend*; 1999; ABC-CLIO Ltd.

Doniger, Wendy (trans); *The Rig Veda*; 1981; Penguin Classics

Gamkrelidze, Tamaz V, and Vjacheslav V. Ivanov; *Indo-European and the Indo-Europeans*; 1995; Mouton de Gruyter

Hudec, Ivan; *Tales from Slavic Myths*; 2001; Bolchazy-Carducci Publishers

Ivanits, Linda J.; *Russian Folk Belief*; 1992; M.E. Sharpe

Kaganskaya, Maya; *The Book of Vles: Saga of a Forgery*; in *Jews and Jewish Topics in Soviet and East-European Publications* 4:3-27 (1986-1987)

Katchur, Viktor (trans); *The Book of Vles*; 1973; Columbus, Ohio

Rybakov, Boris; *Ancient Slavic Paganism*; 1981; Moscow

Sturluson, Snorri; *Prose Edda*; 2002; Everyman

Toporov, Vladimir N.; *Towards the Reconstruction of the Indo-European Rite*; 1982

Warner, Elizabeth; *Russian Myths*; 2002; University of Texas Press; Texas

Warner, Elizabeth; *Heroes, Monsters, and Other Worlds from Russian Mythology*; 1996; Peter Bedrick Books.

ROMANO-CELTIC HORNS

BY ZACHARY YARDLEY

In 1965 the classic work *The Roman Inscriptions of Britain* (RIB) was published, marking a landmark in archaeological collation. This book gathered together all the inscriptions made during the Roman occupation of Britain. Studying such inscriptions reveals much about this occupation of Britain, including some interesting facts about the gods worshipped during this period.

Amongst the inscriptions are ninety-four inscriptions to five horned gods. These horned gods, worshipped by the Celts, were Antenocitus (three), Belatucadros (twenty-six), Camulos (one), Cocidius (twenty-four), and Vitiris (forty).

Significantly all of these inscriptions are from northern England, with one from Scotland. There are none from southern England, which in itself is significant. This absence is slightly reprieved by a plaque found in London in 2002 to the god Mars Camulos. So what do we know about these gods who were significant enough to have their names carved into altars, plaques and statues?

Antenocitus is a god the meaning of whose name is unknown. The remains of a statue of him show a torc and stag horns. He was linked with Mars by the Romans.

Belatucadros means *'Bright Beautiful One'* or *'Fair Shining One'*. The Romans linked him with Mars, and he is several times shown as an armed, ram-horned god. Combined with two references to him with the phrase *'pro se et suis'* (*'for himself and his own'*), this does suggest a protective warrior deity. It has been suggested his origins are Germanic, as legions with Germanic Celts in were based in northern Cumbria, which is where almost all the inscriptions are. The alternative to this is that Belatucadros was a tutelary deity for the Carvetii tribe which ruled that part of England.

Camulos is a ram-horned god whose name means *'the Powerful One'*. He is originally from Belgium, and though there is only one inscription, and a plaque mentioned earlier, coins dedicated to him have also been found around Colchester in Essex, and there are also old place names which were associated with him. These are Camulodunum (meaning *'Fort of Camulos'*), the old name for Colchester; Cambodunum, now Slack in Yorkshire; and Camulosessa (*'Seat of Camulos'*) in southern Scotland. The diversity of references to him makes Camulos probably the most widely worshipped of these horned gods in Britain during the Roman period. He was associated with Mars by the Romans, and the recurring theme of the boar in coins dedicated to him suggests it could have been his sacred animal. It could also indicate that he was a hunting god.

Cocidius may mean *'the Red One'*, though this is uncertain, and based on the suggestion that the name is derived from the Welsh root *'coch'* meaning red. He was worshipped by the Romans as a warrior god, and in this respect was associated with Mars. He was also associated with the Roman forest god Silvanus, probably as a hunting god, as images of him show him hunting animals such as boars, hares and stags. Images also show him with a short cape, spear and shield, which fitted with his role as a soldier god.

Vitiris is a bull-horned god, the meaning of whose name is unknown. It has been suggested the name could be derived from the root *'witsu'* meaning *'knowing'*, and giving a meaning of something like *'the Wise One'*. Alternatively it has also been suggested that the name may come from the old Norse root *'hvitr'* meaning *'shining'* or *'white'*, giving a meaning of something like *'the Shining One'* or *'the White One'*. Vitiris was equated with Mars by the Romans, and seen as both a warrior and hunter god. Images of him showed him armed, and some were also clearly phallic. Uniquely amongst the horned gods there were also triple images of Vitiris, which has led to suggestions he was a type of god and his name was a title, like the Matres (*'Mothers'*) or Nymphs. His association on one inscription with the Celtic god Mogons (*'the Great One'*), who was also worshipped in a multiple form, does also lend credence to this idea. As well as being associated with fertility through the phallic representation, his altars also included bulls and serpents, indicating both fertility and a possible chthonian aspect.

Although not that much is known just from these inscriptions, there are some observations that can be made. Clearly these gods were worshipped and seen as important. They tend to be hunting and/or warrior gods. They have horns, whether they are antlers, bull or ram horns. They are often linked to Mars or another Roman deity, but at the same time most of the inscriptions are to the names without any association to other deities, showing they were not just titles being given to Roman gods, but were Celtic gods in their own right. How much more archaeology will tell us, and how much we can learn from trying to track down these old horned gods and seeing if we can make a good contact is up to us.

Roman Inscriptions relating to the Horned Gods

RIB	Place	County	God
602	Lancaster	Lancashire	Cocidius*
660	York	Yorkshire	Vitiris
727	Brough-by-Baimbridge	Yorkshire	Vitiris*
759	Kirkby Thore	Cumbria	Belatucadros
772	Brougham	Cumbria	Belatucadros
773	Brougham	Cumbria	Belatucadros
774	Brougham	Cumbria	Belatucadros
775	Brougham	Cumbria	Belatucadros
776	Brougham	Cumbria	Belatucadros
777	Brougham	Cumbria	Belatucadros*
809	Maryport	Cumbria	Belatucadros
887	Old Carlisle	Cumbria	Belatucadros*
888	Old Carlisle	Cumbria	Belatucadros*
889	Old Carlisle	Cumbria	Belatucadros
914	Old Penrith	Cumbria	Belatucadros*
918	Old Penrith	Cumbria	Belatucadros
925	Old Penrith	Cumbria	Vitiris
948	Carlise	Cumbria	Belatucadros
966	Netherby	Cumbria	Cocidius*
970	Netherby	Cumbria	Belatucadros
971	Netherby	Cumbria	Vitiris
973	Netherby	Cumbria	Vitiris
985	Bewcastle	Cumbria	Codicius*
986	Bewcastle	Cumbria	Cocidius
987	Bewcastle	Cumbria	Cocidius
988	Bewcastle	Cumbria	Cocidius*
989	Bewcastle	Cumbria	Cocidius*
993	Bewcastle	Cumbria	Cocidius*
1017	Unknown	Cumbria	Cocidius
1046	Chester-le-Street	Durham	Vitiris
1047	Chester-le-Street	Durham	Vitiris
1048	Chester-le-Street	Durham	Vitiris
1087	Lanchester	Durham	Vitiris
1088	Lanchester	Durham	Vitiris
1102	Ebchester	Durham	Cocidius
1103	Ebchester	Durham	Vitiris
1104	Ebchester	Durham	Vitiris
1207	Risingham	Northumberland	Cocidius
1327	Benwell	Tyne-and-Wear	Antenocitus

1328	Benwell	Tyne-and-Wear	Antenocitus
1329	Benwell	Tyne-and-Wear	Antenocitus
1335	Benwell	Tyne-and-Wear	Vitiris*
1336	Benwell	Tyne-and-Wear	Vitiris
1455	Chesters	Northumberland	Vitiris*
1456	Chesters	Northumberland	Vitiris
1457	Chesters	Northumberland	Vitiris
1458	Chesters	Northumberland	Vitiris
1521	Carrawburgh	Northumberland	Belatucadros
1548	Carrawburgh	Northumberland	Vitiris
1549	Carrawburgh	Northumberland	Vitiris
1577	Housesteads	Northumberland	Cocidius
1578	Housesteads	Northumberland	Cocidius
1583	Housesteads	Northumberland	Cocidius
1633	Housesteads	Northumberland	Cocidius
1697	Chesterholm	Northumberland	Vitiris
1698	Chesterholm	Northumberland	Vitiris
1699	Chesterholm	Northumberland	Vitiris
1728	Great Chesters	Northumberland	Vitiris
1729	Great Chesters	Northumberland	Vitiris
1730	Great Chesters	Northumberland	Vitiris
1775	Carvoran	Northumberland	Belatucadros
1776	Carvoran	Northumberland	Belatucadros
1784	Carvoran	Northumberland	Belatucadros
1793	Carvoran	Northumberland	Vitiris
1794	Carvoran	Northumberland	Vitiris
1795	Carvoran	Northumberland	Vitiris*
1796	Carvoran	Northumberland	Vitiris
1797	Carvoran	Northumberland	Vitiris
1798	Carvoran	Northumberland	Vitiris
1799	Carvoran	Northumberland	Vitiris
1800	Carvoran	Northumberland	Vitiris
1801	Carvoran	Northumberland	Vitiris
1802	Carvoran	Northumberland	Vitiris
1803	Carvoran	Northumberland	Vitiris
1804	Carvoran	Northumberland	Vitiris
1805	Carvoran	Northumberland	Vitiris
1872	Birdoswald	Cumbria	Cocidius
1885	Birdoswald	Cumbria	Cocidius
1955	Birdoswald	Cumbria	Cocidius
1956	Birdoswald	Cumbria	Cocidius

1961	Birdoswald	Cumbria	Cocidius
1963	Birdoswald	Cumbria	Cocidius
1976	Castlesteads	Cumbria	Belatucadros
1977	Castlesteads	Cumbria	Belatucadros
2015	Castlesteads	Cumbria	Cocidius
2020	Castlesteads	Cumbria	Cocidius
2024	Castlesteads	Cumbria	Cocidius
2038	Burgh-by-Sands	Cumbria	Belatucadros
2039	Burgh-by-Sands	Cumbria	Belatucadros
2044	Burgh-by-Sands	Cumbria	Belatucadros
2045	Burgh-by-Sands	Cumbria	Belatucadros
2056	Bowness-on-Solway	Cumbria	Belatucadros
2068	Hadrians Wall	Cumbria	Vitiris
2069	Hadrians Wall	Cumbria	Vitiris
2166	Bar Hill	Strathclyde	Camulos

Note an * after the name indicates a reference to the god as
sanctus or *'holy'*.

Bibliography

Collingwood, Prof R.G., & Wright, R.P., *The Roman Inscriptions of Britain - Vol. I Inscriptions on Stone*, 1965, Clarendon Press, Oxford

Goodburn, Roger, & Waugh, Helen; *The Roman Inscriptions of Britain*; 1983; Alan Sutton Publishing Ltd; Gloucester

Henig, Martin, & King, Anthony (eds); *Pagan Gods and Shrines of the Roman Empire*; 1986; Oxford University Committee for Archaeology Monograph No. 8

Keppie, L.J.F., *Roman Inscriptions from Scotland: some additions and corrections to RIB I*, 1983, in Proc Soc Antiq Scot 113:391-404

Pudill, Rainer, & Eyre, Clive, *The Tribes & Coins of Celtic Britain*, 2005, Greenlight Publishing, Essex

THE HORNED SERPENT
BY FRATER NECHESH

"We que moh wee will l'mick,
We que moh m'cha micso,
Som'awo wee will l'mick!
Cardup ke su m'so wo Sawo!

I call on the Wee-Will-l'mick!
I call on the Terrible One!
On the One with the Horns!
I dare him to appear!"
(Algonquin Legends, C.G. Leland, 1884)

The serpent is a creature of contrasts, revered and reviled, bringer of wisdom and temptation. The horned serpent is the same, being viewed in different cultures as a force of great power and conversely of destructive chaos. I have always been fascinated by snakes, so the motif of the horned serpent was one I had to explore. Beyond the initial image of Cernunnos with his ram-headed serpent in Celtic artwork, I soon found horned serpents all around the world. These parallels were often striking in the similarity between very divergent cultures.

The link between Cernunnos and the ram-headed serpent with its horns is well documented. There are two major images on the Gundestrup Cauldron of the ram-headed serpent, one of which shows the connection between the god and the serpent. The size of the serpent in these images implies the divinity of the serpent itself, as well as the god with it. The Val Camonica cave carving in Northern Italy from the fourth century BCE shows a ram-headed serpent with a horned god and an ithyphallic worshipper. Other well known Cernunnos images with the ram-headed serpent include the Autun bronze and the stone statue from Sommerécourt, both in France. Both of these depictions have two ram-horned serpents twined around the waist of Cernunnos, and holding them by the heads in front of himself, feeding them from a patera (i.e. offering plate).

Images found in England further reinforce the link between Cernunnos and the ram-horned serpent. A relief from Cirencester shows a figure of Cernunnos where his legs are replaced with ram-horned serpents, which rear up and have their heads close to his head.

The Roman god Mars was also sometimes associated with the ram-headed serpent in the Romano-Celtic world. As the zodiacal sign associated with Mars is Aries, the ram, this is perhaps no real surprise. A small bronze statue found at Southbroom in Wiltshire shows Mars holding a ram-horned serpent in each hand. At Mavilly in France a Celtic Mars is shown on a stone relief accompanied by a ram-headed serpent.

As previously mentioned, it has been suggested that the ram-headed serpent was seen as a deity itself. Depictions of the serpent without any other obvious deity, such as the plate on the Gundestrup Cauldron where a ram-headed serpent leads a line of warriors, and also two serpents connected with altars. At Lypiatt Park in Gloucestershire an altar was found which had a horned serpent entwined around it. This theme is also seen at Mavilly in France where there is a relief showing a ram-headed serpent entwined around an altar.

The ram-horned or headed serpent appears on torcs and armlets found as grave goods in the Hallstatt C period of Celtic development, i.e. approximately 800-600 BCE. Considering the Roman and Greek references to horned serpents were much later, it is not impossible that there may have been some cross-fertilization of symbolic imagery, particularly as the Celts fought against both the Greeks and the Romans prior to the image occurring in either of their cultures.

The horned serpent appears in Greek myth as a form assumed by Zagreus (*"great hunter"*), the first form of Dionysus before he is dismembered by Titans and his heart used to engender his second birth as Dionysus, son of Zeus. Nonnus in his *Dionysiaca* described the transformations Zagreus underwent as he sought to defend himself:

> *"Sometimes he poured out a whistling hiss from his mouth,*
> *a curling horned serpent covered with scales,*
> *darting out his tongue from his gaping throat,*
> *and leaping upon the grim head of some Titan*
> *encircled his neck in snaky spiral coils."*
> (*Dionysiaca* 6, Nonnus, 5th century CE.)

The cerastes or horned serpent of Libya is mentioned twice by Lucan in *Pharsalia* in the first century CE. Later writers described the cerastes as having four pairs of horns as compared to the usual two found on other horned serpents. This would result in the horned serpent being equated to the biblical devil and the tempting serpent on the tree in the Garden of Eden.

Prior to these serpents was the Egyptian cobra goddess Renenutet (*"She Who Rears"*), commonly shown with a sun disk and horns, or as a woman, or a woman with a snake's head. She was particularly popular amongst agricultural workers, being seen as a fertility deity. From the Middle Kingdom onwards she was particularly venerated, with shrines erected to her in granaries and vineyards especially. Renenutet came to be associated with Isis in the New Kingdom.

Avanyu, great horned winged serpent of the Pueblo Indians is guardian of rains and water sources. Avanyu is clearly paralleled in the Chinese dragon, which also has horns and a serpentine body, and dwells in clouds and guards rains and water sources in a similar manner. Like the Chinese dragon, Avanyu can withhold water, or cause a deluge or even landslide or earthquake if angered. Avanyu was known as Kolowisi to the Zuni tribe and Skatona to the Sia.

Uktena, the horned winged serpent of the Cherokee, had deer antlers, and to see him was said to result in death, even if he was sleeping, though this would then happen to the hunter's family. They had a diamond shaped crest which shone like a star, and hypnotised those who gazed upon it. The Uktenas were more chaotic beings, who tried and failed to kill the Sun. The mortal enemy of Uktena was Tlanuwa the great hawk, which recalls the Indian Garuda, the great eagle which is a mortal enemy to snakes. The Creek also described a similar being, known as a waula, or mazacuate (from the Mexican, literally *"deer-serpent"*). It dwells in lagoons and lakes and cannot be killed by man, only by a direct lightning strike. Like Uktena it is said to make a sound like a rumbling of thunder. This noise from a water spirit is mentioned in the writings of Carlos Castaneda, and may be the source of his inspiration.

The Spiro tribe, an ancient Native American tribe, known for their mound building in what is now Oklahoma, also had images of a creature like the Uktena. Another early tribe who seem to have worshipped a horned serpent deity is the Hopewell People, who were also responsible for large earthworks, this time in Ohio. Figures in slate and mica found at mound sites consistently show depictions of a horned serpent, sometimes connected with altars.

Charles Leland related another similar type of horned serpent in his book *The Algonquin Legends of New England* (1884). The Weewillmekq' was described as being as small as a worm or it could become as large as a horse. It had horns, and could also assume human form. As with other water-dwelling serpent spirits it also had a connection to rain, being able to call storms and attract the thunder and lightning.

Apart from the two horned serpents described by various Native American tribes, a single-horned giant serpent called the Onniont was known to the Huron. His horn could pierce trees, rocks or anything. A piece of the horn was considered a powerful charm which brought great luck to its owner.

As can be seen, the horned serpent turns up all around the world in different forms, both as a force for positive order and disruptive chaos, though more often the former. The combination of the horns of power with the transformative wisdom of the serpent was inevitably going to be popular, and so it should be no surprise that the horned serpent has such an ongoing fascination and appeal.

Bibliography

Duane, O.B.; *Native American Myths & Legends*; 2004; Brockhampton Press Ltd; London

Leland, Charles Godfrey; *The Algonquin Legends of New England*; 1884; Sampson Low, Marston, Searle & Rivington

Lucan; *Pharsalia*; 2007; Echo Library

Nonnus; *Dionysiaca Books 1-15*; 1965; Harvard University Press

Ross, Anne; *Pagan Celtic Britain*; 1967; Routledge & Kegan Paul Ltd; London

Wilkinson, Richard H.; *The Complete Gods and Goddesses of Ancient Egypt*; 2003; Thames & Hudson

BATTLE OF THE BULLS

By Dafydd ap Bran

The *Táin Bó Cúailnge*, or as it is also known, *The Cattle Raid of Cooley*, is one of the great Irish epics, at the heart of the Ulster Cycle of tales. The mythic heart of the whole tale is the rivalry between the two great bulls. The qualities of the bulls are such that they can clearly be seen as divine beings. Moreover these bulls have a long history, as the tales recount the rivalry between the two souls which ended up as the bulls.

The bulls started off as two swineherds called Fruich (*'bristle'*) and Rucht (*'grunt'*), who worked for two fairy kings (i.e. gods) Ochall and Bodb. The men were friends, and both were competent magicians, able to shift their shape into any animal. However as is often the way, other people who were jealous of their friendship set them against each other. The result of this was an ongoing conflict which saw them take a number of different animal shapes, culminating in the mighty bulls, horned animal lords.

The sequence of animals they transform through is interesting and revealing. Each shape is taken for two years, before shifting to the next one. This seems to represent a year culminating in a win for each of the opponents, so it is always eventually a stalemate.

The first shape they take is of two arguing birds of prey, Ingen ('*talon*') and Ette ('*wing*'), which caw at each other for two years.

Next they became underwater creatures, Bled ('*whale*') and Blod ('*seabeast*') and devoured each other. The third transformation was as stags with herds of deer, then two warriors, Rinna ('*point*') and Faebur ('*edge*') who injured each other. Then they became two phantoms Scath ('*shadow*') and Sciath ('*shield*'), and then two dragons. From the dragons they became worms, which were swallowed by cows that gave birth to the mighty bulls.

It is interesting to note that after having transformed through all of the elements of Air (ravens), Fire (dragons), Water (water creatures), Earth (stags) and Ethereal (phantoms), the two resort to the humblest of forms to be transformed by the cows, suggesting a rebirth through the earth goddess (cow) which they could not achieve through their magick.

The two mighty bulls were Finnbennach Ai, the White, and Donn Cuailnge, the Brown. Whilst the Cattle Raid of Cooley revolves around possession of the mighty bulls, it is the bulls themselves which are the focus of this piece. Although Finnbennach is called white, in fact he is described as having a white head and feet and a red body. Red and white are the otherworldly colours in Celtic mythology, so this is clearly emphasising his magickal nature.

The magickal nature of the bulls is repeatedly emphasised. Thus the subsequent conflict is provoked by the Morrigan in crow form sitting on a rock near the Brown Bull and prophesying the attempts to kidnap him which are central to the saga of the Táin. That he should understand the goddess is not even considered, and the way she speaks to him is almost as a meeting of equals.

The magickal virtues of the Brown Bull are listed and indicate his great size. He is credited with the following attributes:

- He could cover fifty heifers a day;
- Fifty grown youths could play games on his back;
- One hundred warriors could shelter from the heat and cold in his shadow and under him;
- When he drinks from a river no water passes as long as he drinks;
- No goblin, sprite or boggart dared come near him;
- The music of his lowing in the evening would delight all men who heard it.

That no mischievous spirits could come near to him and the musical nature of his lowing both emphasise his divine roots.

The bulls fought for a night and a day, killing one of the onlookers, until the Brown Bull triumphed. He is described as coming from the west with torn fragments of Finnbennach hanging over his horns and ears. As the Brown Bull then triumphantly travels across the land bits of the dead white bull fall off him, after which the places were named. This naming of the places after Finnbennach hints at his role having been more subsumed in the tale, and the emphasis on his divinity being mainly seen through these names.

When the two bulls are described the contrast between them is emphasised by the animals they are likened to. The Brown Bull is likened to a lion and a bear and a bull, Finnbennach is likened to a stallion, a cow and a salmon. The former has his martial qualities brought to the fore by the comparisons, whereas the latter has his versatility emphasised.

The contrast between the powers of the two bulls is also demonstrated in the titles given to them. Whilst the Brown bull is called the *'Father of the great beasts'*, Finnbennach is called *'the prime demon'*. This almost smacks of a Christian layer being added, with the Brown Bull clearly being viewed more positively.

Place Name	Named after
Cruachan Ai	A heap (cruach) of liver from Finnbennach
Sruthair Finnlethe	The shoulderblades (lethe) of Finnbennach
Athione	The loin (luan) of Finnbennach
Ath Truim	The liver (tromm) of Finnbennach
Port Large	The hind leg (lárac) of Finnbennach
Ath Cliath (Dublin)	The ribs (clíathac) of Finnbennach

The tale ends with a twist, as on returning home the Brown Bull goes on a killing rampage amongst women and children who were mourning him, believing him dead. After killing them all his heart breaks apart in his chest and he dies. Thus the two swineherds end up dying close to each other, reunited in death as they once were in friendship. It is clear that these mighty bulls are remnants of an earlier horned god tale, and these hints can only give us a glimpse of what was probably a conflict tale representing light and dark or the two halves of the year.

Further Reading
Kinsella, Thomas (trans); *The Tain*; 1970; Oxford University Press; Oxford
Mallory, J.P. (ed); *Aspects of the Tain*; 1992; December Publications; Belfast
O'Rahilly, Cecil (ed); *Táin Bó Cúailnge from The Book of Leinster*; 1967; Dublin Institute for Advanced Studies, Dublin
O'Rahilly, Cecil (ed); *Táin Bó Cúailnge Recension I*; 1976; Dublin Institute for Advanced Studies, Dublin

PUCK: FORGOTTEN DEVIL GOD?

BY BETH RAVEN

Of all the characters we encounter in British folklore, few have been both as mentioned in literature and as belittled as Puck. The origins of Puck are not clear, though the descriptions of him sometimes liken him to Pan, with goat's feet and legs. Descriptions however vary, as does his name, depending on where in Britain you travel to. Thus he is also Pwcca in Wales, Bwca or Bucca in Cornwall, Pooka in Ireland and a whole host of variants on the name such as Phooka, Pooken and Puca. Some describe him as a mischievous nature spirit who would lead people astray, curdle milk or try and molest maidens, whilst other maidens called on him for revenge on lovers who had spurned them. Everywhere we look, Puck is full of contradictions. Thus the hairy spirit of Wales might be encountered wearing a green suit in Southern England. Perhaps the shape-shifting trickster nature of Puck is the real indicator, Puck represents a force that cannot be neatly categorised and put in a box.

The name *'Puck'* sounds a great deal better than the derogatory term devil used so frequently during the Middle Ages and Renaissance to describe anything with horns, which is probably why that great English bard, Shakespeare used the term *"Sweet Puck"* with such wonderful mirth in *A Midsummer Night's Dream*, where we find the Fairy speaking to Puck saying:

> *"Either I mistake your shape and making quite,*
> *Or else you are that shrewd and knavish sprite*
> *Call'd Robin Goodfellow: are not you he*
> *That frights the maidens of the villagery;*
> *Skim milk, and sometimes labour in the quern*
> *And bootless make the breathless housewife churn;*
> *And sometime make the drink to bear no barm;*
> *Mislead night-wanderers, laughing at their harm?*
> *Those that Hobgoblin call you and sweet Puck,*
> *You do their work, and they shall have good luck:*
> *Are not you he?"*

(*A Midsummer Night's Dream*, William Shakespeare)

Shakespeare was not the only English author to include Puck in his writing. The Irish bard Thomas Moore (1779-1852) wrote an entire piece featuring Puck and entitled *The Legend of Puck the Fairy:*

> *Wouldst know what tricks, by pale moonlight,*
> *Are play'd by me, the merry little Sprite,*
> *Wh wint thrugh air from the camp to court,*
> *From king to clown, and of all make sport;*
> *Singing, I am the Sprite*
> *Of the merry midnight,*
> *Who laugh at weak mortals, and love the moonlight.*

> *To a miser's bed, where he snoring slept,*

And dreamt of his cash, I slily crept,;
Chink, chink o'er his pillow like money I rang,
And he waked to catch - but away he sprang,
Singing, I am the Sprite, &c.

I saw through the leaves, in a damsel's bower,
She was waiting her love at that starlight hour:
"Hist - hist!" quoth I, with an amorous sigh,
And she flew to the door, but away flew I,
Singing, I am the Sprit, &c.

While a bard sat inditing an ode to his love,
Like a pair of blue meters I star'd from above,
And he swoon'd - for he thought 'twas the ghost,
poor man!
Of his lady's eyes, while away I ran,
Singing, I am the Sprite, &c.

So why is Puck in a book about Horned Gods? Well, firstly it is important to be clear that our views on Puck have likely been coloured by those conveyed by Shakespeare in *A Midsummer Night's Dream*. Shakespeare actually lightened the tone of much of what was perceived about Puck prior to his work. Shakespeare made Puck a member of the fairy court, from being a loner who might mislead people in the wilds, and make them Pouk-ledden (misled). Other writers picked up on this, as can be seen in the *Nymphedia* of Michael Drayton (1627), where Puck is a member of the fairy court who serves King Oberon.

Then we also need to be clear that Puck may not currently be a *'god'* in the sense that is usually understood, but that in fact he is a mischievous fairy creature. Whether he was originally viewed as a god is not something that can be easily determined, as the evidence is lacking, though the fact he was likened to Pan and equated with the devil might lean towards this conclusion, based on the notion that the gods of yesterday become the devils of today. He is very universal in his appearance though, and writing in *Hobgoblin and Sweet Puck* the author Gillian Edwards states:

> *"Parallel words exist in many ancient languages – puca in Old English, puki in Old Norse, puke in Swedish, puge in Danish, puks in Low German, pukis in Latvia and Lithuania – mostly with he original meaning of a demon, devil, evil and malignant spirit. The Celtic tongues have it too; in Irish puca and pucca in Welsh."*

This idea of Puck as a devil is seen in the fourteenth century when Langland equated Puck with the Devil in *Piers the Ploughman* and called hell *"Pouk's Pinfold"*. This idea was continued by Spenser in his *Epithalamion* (1597), where he wrote:

> *"Ne let the Pouke, nor other evil sprights,*
> *Ne let mischievous witches with theyr charmes."*

Although Robert Burton in his *Anatomy of Melancholy* in 1638 had talked about *'a Puck'* as a class of creature, the earlier works of others like Spenser, Langland and Shakespeare had already served to give him a more singular character, removed from the idea of a type of being.

But our story continues with Puck as the possible source of the image old Hornie himself, the Devil of the Christian people, that is. Certainly it seems that for some he was a prime suspect of all things evil and bad. In that wonderfully witchy county of Sussex, *"Pook"* as he is called there, is remembered as being a *'goatsucker'* (nightjar) as well as the disease given by these birds to cattle, according to Edwards writing in *Hobgoblin and Sweet Puck*.

"this Puck seems but a dreaming dolt;
Still walking like a ragged colt,
And oft out of a bush doth bolt,
Of purpose to deceive us;
And, leaving us, makes us to stray,
Long winter nights, out of the way;
And when we stick in mire and clay;
He doth with laughter leave us."
(*Polyolbion*, by Drayton)

In the image to the left, a woodcut from the 1847 edition of the *Roxburge Ballads*, based on an earlier image from a 17th century publication, Puck or Robin Goodfellow, as he is also sometimes known (following on from Shakespeare's connection of the two), is clearly shown with horns and with other imagery linking him to witchcraft. He holds a broom in his left hand, a torch in his right, there is a circle of witches dancing about him and much merriment indicated by the music and wine jug in the forefront. So could Puck provide an antecedent for the Horned God found in today's witchcraft? Certainly based on imagery such as this, it would seem possible!

"While Angus was talking a Pooka came out from between the trees. It looked like a little snow-white kid with golden horns and silver hoofs, but it could take any shape it had a fancy for..."
(*Celtic Wonder Tales*, by Ella Young)

In Ireland, the Pooka is probably amongst the most feared of the little people. Like all monsters he seems to emerge from within the darkness of night and is able to shapeshift according to myth, into a number of different forms. The horse was a particular favourite form, though not for the people who saw him as he could be an omen of death. This of course gives him a distinct advantage when it comes to tricking people and creating havoc. As a result of this, in parts of the rural areas, pooka's share is still left at the end of the harvest, to placate him, for luck and to ensure a good harvest the next year – whether he appears as a eagle or as a goat with grotesquely big horns, Pooka seems to be very much a creature associated with the land, the Earth itself, which is what you would expect from a Horned God. In fact his name in some languages can be translated as earth spirit which again makes you wonder about the Horned God and his associations with the forests and glades – and of course the Horned God is sometimes associated with the fairy folk.

As a will-o-the-wisp he demonstrates his trickster side. He would lead travellers up narrow paths to the edge of a ravine, leap over and laughing, blow out his candle, leaving the traveller in the dark. This does recall the Fool of the Tarot however, and make one think of the initiatory imagery associated with this apparent trickery.

A story from Wales shows Puck, or rather Pwca, in his role as a brownie. Every day a milkmaid would leave a bowl of milk and a piece of white bread out for him, until one day she drank the milk and ate most of the bread, leaving water and a crust for Pwca. The next day as she approached a pair of invisible sharp hands gave her a thorough whipping and she was warned that next time she would receive worse treatment. This role of helpful spirit (brownie) is one he is found in around the British Isles, though his trickster side was never far away.

Kipling's take on Puck is interesting, as he describes him as being immune to all of the charms which were used to protect from fairy. Kipling is clearly hinting that Puck was more than a simple fairy creature:

"Sprinkle a plenty salt on the biscuit, Dan, and I'll eat it with you. That'll show you the sort of person I am. Some of us' – he went on, with his mouth full – 'couldn't abide Salt, or Horse-shoes over a door, or Mountain-ash berries, or Running Water, or Cold Iron, or the sound of Church Bells. But I'm Puck."

(*Puck of Pook's Hill*, Rudyard Kipling)

Whichever your Puck and where ever you may encounter him, remember be polite, smile and share your food and drink with him to have him as a friend. Better a friend than an enemy with a creature whose morals are so uncertain. He may appear small and unimportant, but that is all part of his charm.

Bibliography
Briggs, Katharine; *A Dictionary of Fairies*; 1977; Penguin Books; Harmondsworth
Briggs, Katharine; *The Anatomy of Puck*; 1977; Routledge & Kegan Paul; London
Burton, Robert; *The Anatomy of Melancholy*; 1638; London
Edwards, Gillian; *Hobgoblin and Sweet Puck*; 1974; Geoffrey Bles; London
Kipling, Rudyard; *Puck of Pook's Hill*; 1906; Macmillan; London
Linden, Stanton J.; *Darke Hierogliphicks: Alchemy in English Literature from Chaucer to the Restoration*; 1996; University of Kentucky Press; Kentucky

Khnum by Nina Falaise

THE POTTER FROM THE NILE

By Sorita d'Este

As one of the oldest of the Egyptian gods, Khnum has always fascinated me. His origins are lost in the pre-dynastic period, usually shown in semi-anthropomorphic form with a human body and long-horned ram head, wearing a long tripartite wig and a short kilt. Khnum was particularly associated with the first cataract of the river Nile, and he was said to control the inundation of the Nile from its source. As such he was very much seen as a fertility god, and this connection to the Nile with its fertile black mud may have contributed to his worship as a potter god, forming life on his wheel.

"Khnum, maker of all, spin the wheel of life and breathe your creative power into my words and deeds; infuse my ka with the might of your ba."

Khnum's role as a fertility god connected with the Nile is seen in the so-called *'Famine Stela'*. This carving from the Ptolemaic Period on the island of Sehel near Aswan contained a prayer to Khnum asking him to end the famine caused by seven years of low inundations. Khnum subsequently appeared in a dream to King

Djoser, telling him that he would let the river flood and the famine would end, which indeed it did.

As well as making the bodies of everyone on his potter's wheel, Khnum also infused them with their *ka* (life force). Khnum was even credited in some texts with forming the bodies of the gods themselves, and with the creation of the first egg, from which the sun god Ra was born.

Khnum also appeared in a dream to reveal the legendary book of magic known as the *Book of Thoth* (no relation to the Tarot). A Nubian sorceror worked magic against the Pharaoh Siamun, taking him to Nubia and beating him with 500 strokes in front of the Nubian ruler. An understandably annoyed Siamun summoned his own magicians and priests, and a scribe called Horus went to the temple of Khnum and asked for aid. Whilst sleeping in the temple awaiting a magical dream, Khnum appeared to him in his dream and told him where the magic book was hidden in a sealed chamber of the temple library. Once the book was retrieved it was a simple matter to use a spell in it to return the compliment and beat the Nubian ruler!

"Lord of the Wheel, who fashioned gods and men, mould the substance of my dream and reveal the truth, guide my actions that I may do only true deeds."

As a ram-headed god, Khnum was long-horned, though some later images show him with shorter horns. In a classic Egyptian play on words, the word for ram is *'ba'*, which is also the personality part of the soul. Khnum was described as being the ba of several of the gods, notably the solar creator god Ra, the earth god Geb and the underworld god Osiris. His name was joined with that of Ra to give the composite god Khnum-Ra, a ram-headed form of Ra often seen on the solar barque travelling through the underworld. This is because the soul (ba) of Ra is being depicted, so it is commonly shown in the ram form of Khnum. Some images of Khnum show him with a quadruple ram's head, with the four heads representing himself, Ra, Geb and Osiris. The underworld connection is also seen in the engravings of Khnum found on heart scarabs, as he was often invoked for protection and aid in the judgement of the soul in the hall of Maat.

"Fourfold god of sun, earth, water and underworld, having power in all realms, protect me as I travel to my destination."

Khnum was linked to several different goddesses. At different times he was linked to the primal frog-headed creatrix Heqet, and he was also associated with Satis and Anuket. Although this latter association at his cult centre of Elephantine could be either as wife and daughter, or as two wives, what is more significant is their natures. Satis was connected with the antelope and her crown bore antelope horns, and Anuket was associated with the gazelle, where the male of the species also bears horns. So there is a strong horned connection in the wives of Khnum as well. Satis with her arrows defended people, and Anuket with her life-giving milk nourished them. Together with Khnum they make a strong triad.

"Khnum, bless my child with your creative power and form him whole and healthy; Satis protect him from all infirmity with your striking arrows; Anuket nurture him and ensure the waters of life always flow to him."

Khnum was often depicted in a fully zoomorphic form as a walking ram, but as many images do not have complete accompanying inscriptions it can be very difficult to tell. However we do know he was often inscribed on pectorals and the scarabs which were placed over the heart. He was also known as the 'Lord of the Crocodiles' in his role as Lord of the Nile. In this role he was sometimes associated with the early war goddess Neith, and on occasion was seen as the father of her son Sobek, the crocodile god.

Khnum was also said to have created the first labour-saving device, and ironically it is the device which produces labour, i.e. the womb! After many years of creating life, Khnum was said to have got tired, so he placed a smaller version of his potter's turn-table in every womb of every female creature, transmitting his creative power to the females of all the species. Khnum then was able to concentrate on maintaining the creation of the life force (ka).

"Potter God, Maker of All, Lord of the Crocodiles,
Ba of the Gods, Mighty Khnum
You I adore, you I praise, to you I offer pure food and drink
My heart is pure, accept my offerings."

Bibliography
Badawi, A.M.; *Der Gott Chnum*; 1937; Glückstadt
Hornung, Erik; *Conceptions of God in Ancient Egypt*; 1996; Cornell University Press; New York
Pinch, Geraldine; *Magic in Ancient Egypt*; 1994, British Museum Press; London
Pinch, Geraldine; *Egyptian Mythology*; 2002; Oxford University Press; Oxford
Rankine, David; *Heka: The Practices of Ancient Egyptian Ritual & Magic*; 2006; Avalonia; London
Watterson, Barbara; *The Gods of Ancient Egypt*; 1984; B.T. Batsford Ltd; London
Wilkinson, Richard H.; *The Complete Gods and Goddesses of Ancient Egypt*; 2003; Thames & Hudson; London

HORNS FROM EGYPT
By Phil Lightwood-Jones

One might argue that ancient Egypt did not have a horned God. There is a view that Egyptians considered their Gods to be superhuman or supercharged beings. The portrayal of Egyptian deities with animal components or as full animals was only useful shorthand to help them understand the different aspects of their Gods which is why many Gods were depicted in several different forms. For example, a God with the attributes of a bull meant strength and fertility, a ram because of its procreative vigour and so on. This approach leads to the logical conclusion that the image was not the God but an icon of an attribution of the God. In later times it is true that Egyptians worshipped certain animals as Gods but this may be because they lost touch with the original meaning. This is hardly surprising; the origins of the Gods go back to dimly distant prehistoric times and may lie forever beyond our understanding.

One of our earliest extant depictions of ancient Egyptian horned deities can be found on the Narmer palette. A cow headed deity (presumably female) tops the palette and a bull is shown breaking down a city wall and trampling an enemy. The bull may be a reference to the king, one of whose epithets was *"strong bull"* or it may be of a God or an aspect of a God. A different perspective, and the very earliest evidence tends to uphold this view, is that Gods were not shown as humans at all in Egypt's earliest periods. Crudely formed anthropomorphic figures from the Naqada period have been interpreted as deities although it is far from certain that they are divine representations. It is not until the beginning of the historical period can we say with complete certainty that hybrid forms were used to represent their Gods.

The Egyptians drew the God down from His celestial realm and invited Him to reside in it's image – for example, at the temple of Horus at Edfu, Horus was invited daily to reside in the image of the Sacred Falcon and was revered, fed and clothed, so it is clear that the Falcon, in this case, was the God, suggesting that the image was more than simply a shorthand way of understanding the attributes associated with a deity.

Bovine deities were extremely important to the ancient Egyptians and epitomized both male and female deities, but we are concerned here only with the male Gods. Male bovine deities generally possessed great power and sexual potency which led them to be equated with kingship but they also possessed cosmic attributions. Ovine deities were almost exclusively male ram-Gods and were usually found in specific geographical sites, Khnum and Elephantine being the best known. The Egyptian fondness for wordplay meant that they often equated the translation of *"ram"* (ba) with *"spirit"* (ba) and worshipped them as the ba of important Gods such as Re or Osiris.

If one includes the *"horns"* of the crescent moon it may be possible to include the moon as a horned deity although it is far from certain that the moon was actually worshipped as a deity per se. It is more likely that the moon was representative of certain aspects of a deity so the moon has been excluded from this listing.

Iah is an example of a moon God. He is a lunar God whose name translates as *"moon"* and he has been depicted with crescent moon symbols.

A-Z of the Horned Egyptian Gods: Reference Guide

Amun, Amun Re, Amun Kamutef, Amun Min

The ram is associated with Amun and he is often shown as a ram or ram headed deity. Amun Kamutef is translated as Amun, bull of his mother. Amun was also associated with lions and criosphinxes representing him a ram headed lions can be seen at Karnak temple.

Anubis, Anup

Anubis is predominantly associated with funerary and afterlife concerns and is usually depicted in a canine form, often as a jackal, and is master of the per wabet, the place where embalming took place. In the tomb of Seti I, Anubis is shown with a ram's head.

Apis

Apis was the most important of the bull Gods and while we often think of the Apis bull as being associated with later times he was, in fact, evident right from the start of the dynastic era. The origins may be linked with an ancient God called Hap. The Greek historian Herodotus tells us that Apis was always black with very particular wing or hawk-like markings on its body and a white triangle on its forehead. Apis is most commonly depicted as a walking or standing bull but there are rare images of him as a bull headed man. Apis was famed for his oracles.

Atum

The cult of Atum is very ancient. He was the great primeval deity of Heliopolis and his most essential characteristic is that of *"self engendered one"*. Atum has strong chthonic and underworld connections. He is occasionally depicted as a ram headed God and in this guise he is most strongly associated with the underworld. Atum is also found as a bull which connects him directly with the Egyptian kings.

Baal

The Western Semitic storm god was accepted in ancient Egypt because aspects of his story are similar to the resurrection myth associated with Osiris. His pugnacious nature also equated him with Seth. Baal's cult animal was the bull and he is often depicted wearing a conical, funnel-like helmet with two horns at its base.

Banebdjedet

"Banebdjedet" means *"the ba (or power) of the Lord of Djedet"*. Djedet is the city of Mendes. Banebdjedet had strong sexual power and is represented as a ram or ram headed man, though occasionally he is shown as just the head of the ram. In some New Kingdom images he is shown with four heads to symbolize the four gods with whom he is closely associated, Re, Osiris, Shu and Geb.

Bes

After the third intermediate period we find images of Bes syncretised with multiple deities, some of whom had horns, but Bes in his purest form cannot be considered to be truly a horned God.

Buchis

A bull deity, Buchis (in Egyptian bakh, ba-akh or bakhu) is often confused with Apis and like Apis, had particular markings to identify him but because of confusion about the nature of these markings it is often difficult to identify him. Buchis was famous for delivering oracles and curing diseases (particularly those of the eye). He is connected with Re, Osiris and especially Montu.

Dedwen

Dedwen was originally a Nubian deity but recognised in Egypt from at least the Old Kingdom. He has many attributions, one of which is the horned ram when he is assimilated with Amun or Khnum. Dedwen was the supplier of incense for the Gods and burnt incense at royal births.

Heryshef

This God's name translates as *"he who is on his lake"*, suggesting he may have been regarded as a creator God rising from the primordial waters but may also have referred to his sacred lake at his cult centre of Hnes (Herakleopolis Magna). He is connected with Osiris and Re and the Greeks linked him with Herakles. He is allied with Atum through his association with the sacred naret tree of Hnes. Heryshef is often shown as a man with distinctly long ram's horns and his associations with Osiris means he is also shown as a ram or ram-headed man wearing the *"Atef"* crown or with the sun disk of the Sun God as a result of his links with Re.

Kherty

This ram-God is a chthonic deity whose name means *"lower one"* suggesting that he inhabits the netherworld. Kherty has a dual nature; he is capable of both hostility and protection and is described in the Pyramid Texts (PT 1308) as *"the chin of the king"*.

His association with Osiris led to his being regarded as a protector of the king's tomb but in PT 350 Re must protect the king from Kherty. Normally we find Kherty in the guise of a ram and associated with Khnum we also find him as a bull or lion and in any of his forms he may also be equated with Re.

Khnum

Khnum is an important ram headed deity associated particularly with the Nile and the creation of life. He controlled the inundation from the caverns of the region of the first cataract. In his incarnation as a potter he shaped all living things on his wheel. He is associated with Re, Geb, Osiris Neith and Menhyt. He can also be depicted as the first species  of sheep to be bred in Egypt, Ovis longipes with its horizontal, undulating horns, and, of course, as Ovis platyra, the Amun Ram with its short, curved horns. In some depictions he may have two sets of horns. Where he is depicted in his zoomorphic form as a walking ram he can be confused with Heryshef.

Khonsu

A moon God often shown wearing his symbol of the full moon resting in the crescent new moon on his head, which may be construed as horned.

Mandulis

A solar God who wears rams horns, sun disks and cobras topped by plumes.

Min

An ancient and long standing deity, Min was God of the eastern desert and of male sexual procreativity and fertility. Usually recognised in the form of an ithyphallic mummy or tightly wrapped man with black skin Min is also depicted as a white bull.

Mnevis

Mnevis was the divine bull of Heliopolis and in Egyptian is mer-wer or nem-wer. Mnevis was the divine ba or power of Re and was the herald of the sun God making his wishes known in the form of oracles. Heliopolitan priests claimed that Mnevis was the father of Apis.

Neferhotep

This child deity is known as the son of Hathor and has been depicted as a divine ram. He was both the child and the power behind the child's conception.

Osiris

Osiris is an extremely important deity about which much is already written. The cult of Osiris lasted for over 2,000 years and was already well established by the end of the fifth dynasty. The origins of his name are not certain but recent studies suggest that it may mean *"mighty one"* from the Egyptian *useru*. He was probably originally a fertility God with strong chthonic connections and was probably associated at some point with the Nile's inundation. His most recognisable image is that of a human mummy but his syncretised form when fused with Re is shown as a mummy with the head of a falcon, beetle or ram.

Ptah

This deity is only shown with rams horns in his syncretised form such as Ptah-Sokar-Osiris, when he wears the horns of a ram.

Re

Most associated with the falcon Re can also be seen as a ram or ram headed man or a bull. He is frequently fused with other animals as a composite God.

Reshep

Reshep was the west Semitic God of war and thunder and was brought into the Egyptian pantheon along with arrange of other Near Eastern deities during the New Kingdom. He was especially associated with Set and Montu. Reshep is frequently shown with the horns or full head of a gazelle, perhaps indicating his desert origins.

Sepa

One of the more surprising of Egypt's Horned Gods, Sepa, *"the Centipede of Horus"* is known from the Old Kingdom right through to Graeco Roman times. Sepa has also been represented as a donkey-headed man and as a mummy with two short horns on his head.

Serapis

Serapis was a composite deity consisting of several Egyptian and Hellenistic gods and is a late introduction into the Egyptian pantheon, probably during the reign of Ptolemy I although a cult of

Osirapis (a union of Osiris and Apis) existed before the Ptolemies. Serapis undoubtedly emerged from of this Egyptian deity when aspects of Zeus, Hades, Dionysus, Helios and Asklepius were incorporated. Apis is, of course, the most important bull deity in the Egyptian pantheon and we have dealt with him earlier. Serapis carries the bull's characteristics through his origins as Osirapis but is also depicted with curving ram's horns.

Set

While not normally associated with a horned animal there are rare depictions of Set as an antelope and a goat.

Shezmu

Shezmu (Shesmu) has a strongly bipolar personality and is equally attested as a God who could bless or destroy. He was the God of oil and wine presses and his most well known representation is from the so called *"Cannibal Hymn"* of the *Pyramid Texts* (PT 403). One hieroglyph associated with Shesmu is that of the wine press. Apart from his fierce role of butchering and cooking the Gods so that the king might take in their strength. In his role as butcher he is sometimes called *"Lord of the Slaughterhouse of Horus"*. He is also perfumer to the Gods. Shesmu was particularly beneficent to the dead and during the Middle Kingdom was often regarded as God of the wine press, a role he later swaps, during the early New Kingdom for that of supreme ointment maker. At Dendera and Edfu he is given the title *"Lord of the Laboratory"*. Throughout Egyptian history, however, Shesmu has the enduring representation as a butcher, and his iconography will often indicate a dual role for the deity. In the *Coffin Texts* demons known as *"the Shesmus"* assisted him in his cruel endeavours. He is shown with ram's horns in late representations but not in earlier times. There is a particularly interesting study of Shesmu the Letopolite in *Studies in Honor of George R Hughes* (1977, Studies in Ancient Oriental Civilization No 39) by Mark Ciccarello. Shesmu appears as early as the *Pyramid Texts* and endures throughout Egyptian civilisation until Graeco-Roman times. In the *Pyramid Texts* we find Shesmu as affable, bringing wine for the dead king and, in the *"Cannibal Hymn"* he butchers the Gods, placing them in a cauldron. He is associated with a scene of the grape harvest in a Saqqara tomb where youths can be seen playing a ritual game labelled *sti Ssmw*, *"shooting for? Shesmu"*. There may have been an Old Kingdom priesthood devoted to Shesmu. Associations with Shesmu include the cauldron (*ktwt*), the *"peg"* (*mxsf*) of the net and his *"calf"* (*sbq*), the knife (*mds*), and thighs (*iwa .wy*). The cauldron of Shesmu is associated with *"woman"* and the knife of Shesmu with man while the thighs of Shesmu are associate with oars. See Ciccarellos excellent study referred to earlier for further details about this and many other aspects of this deity.

Sky Bull

Also known as *"Bull of the West"* the sky bull features in Chapter 148 of the *Book of the Dead* as a mythical creature or deity associated with the heavens and the afterlife. He was the husband to seven cows which may represent *"the seven Hathors"*. The Sky Bull is depicted in the tomb of Nefertari.

Sobek

Sobek's origins lie as far back as the Old Kingdom and possibly earlier. As the son of Neith he is called in the *Pyramid Texts* *"the raging one"* who *"takes women from their husbands.* He is also associated with vegetation and fertility and as a crocodile is, unsurprisingly, a water God. Sobek is sometimes shown as a man with the head of a crocodile or as a crocodile seated on a throne. He often wears a plumed headpiece with sun disk and horns. He is closely associated with the colour green and one of his titles is *"green of plume"*.

Tatanen

Tatanen is a Memphite God who is first fully attested from the Middle Kingdom but may be associated with or even be the same deity as the much earlier Khenty-Tjenet. He is also connected with Ptah and Geb. His name means *"risen land"* and this puts him firmly in the context of primeval creator deities. He may be a bisexual deity; he has been referred to as *"creator and mother of all the Gods"* in at least one text. He is also viewed as the personification of the phallus of the king (perhaps a word-play deriving from the meaning of his name). He wears a headdress of a sun disk with ram's horns and plumes.

Bibliography
Assmann, Jan; *The Search for God in Ancient Egypt*; 2001; Cornell University Press; Ithaca
Frankfort, Henri; *Ancient Egyptian Religion, and interpretation*; 1975 (first pub 1948); Dover; New York
Hart, George; *The Routledge Dictionary of Egyptian Gods and Goddesses*; 2005; Routledge; London
Wilkinson, Richard H.; *The Complete Gods and Goddesses of Ancient Egypt*; 2003; Thames and Hudson; London

HORN OF THE UNICORN

By Janet Nancy James

"Will the unicorn be willing to serve thee,
or abide by thy crib?
Canst thou bind the unicorn with his band in the furrow?
Or will he harrow the valleys after thee?
Wilt thou trust him,
because his strength is great?
Or wilt thou leave thy labour to him?
Wilt thou believe him,
that he will bring home thy seed,
and gather it into thy barn?"
(Job 39:9-12)

This quote from the Old Testament was my introduction to the mighty unicorn. I was intrigued and from that moment onwards wanted to know all about this strong and untamed creature that was new to me. I scoured my bible, yes, an eight year old girl obsessed with reading her bible looking for any other references I could find. My hunt was quickly fruitful, as I discovered numerous references to the unicorn and his horn as well as lots of really grim stuff that eight year olds shouldn't read. Man, the Bible should have an eighteen rating with all the violence and abuse that goes on in it!

Anyhow, I quickly found a reference in *Numbers*, and then another in *Deuteronomy*, which gave me hope, as nothing in the first few books would probably have resulted in my attention being distracted elsewhere. But no, I quickly discovered that *"God brought him forth out of Egypt; he hath as it were the strength of an unicorn"* (*Numbers 24:8*) and *"His horns are like the horns of unicorns: with them he shall push the people together to the ends of the earth"* (*Deuteronomy 33:17*).

Psalms, Isaiah, Daniel, the list went on, and I knew I had found the horn of power, as *Psalm 92:10* said, *"But my horn shalt thou exalt like the horn of an unicorn."* After the bible I started looking elsewhere, spending hours in the local library, to the amazement and delight of my parents. Here I discovered the magnificent and beautiful unicorns of the Orient. The oriental unicorn is one of the four sacred animals, symbolising the element of Earth. It is more than this though, as can be seen by its association with the five sacred colours of blue, red, yellow, white and black – the primary colours and the twin poles of reflection (white) and absorption (black). The oriental unicorn embodies all the noble qualities, its voice sounds like a bell (heaven) and it does not harm any living creature or plant. Unicorns are seen when a good ruler is in power, and noticeably absent when a bad one rules. The hint here is the old adage of *"the king and the land are one"*, for the unicorn surely embodies the power of the land more than any other creature.

I wondered if there was more of a connection between the dragon and the unicorn. After all in the Orient they were both sacred creatures. Sure enough I discovered there was, in the Babylonian myths. The unicorn was one of the eleven types of monster created by the primal goddess Tiamat to fight the hero-god Marduk. These children of Tiamat were described as deities, so the unicorn was indeed originally a god, as I had hoped. By this time I was a bit obsessed with unicorns, with pictures all over my walls and statues on my shelves. I would hasten to add that I drew the pictures and the statues were poor attempts made by my from clay, not the mass-produced New Age virgin fluffy unicorns that have since filled the market with their nauseating candy corn emasculated horn.

The Babylonian unicorn was described as bad, but only if you considered hero types who get away with murder to be good (see that bible reading really did have an influence on me). I am the sort of person who will cheer for the chaos bringer, forget the government licensed killer who is considered noble, give me the honest villain every time.

The unicorn as popularly seen today probably comes from the Zoroastrian religion, where it is portrayed as being as big as a mountain with a huge gold horn, and it purifies everywhere it goes and wipes out the evil creatures. Thus was born the golden horned virtuous creature of good. However in the original stories he is the essence of virility, impregnating the feminine waters and causing mass births of young in animals and being portrayed next to a tree of life. As I said, the New Age supported the whole Christian idea of chastity, that only a virgin could approach and tame a unicorn. Excuse me? Here is this divine beast with a huge horn, and you think a virgin is going to tame him with her innocence? Come on, get real! He wants an orgy, he is permanently ready for it! Also he is mountain-sized, this is a divine creature by any standards.

Classical writers recorded a great deal of information on how they perceived the unicorn, which has also influenced the modern view. If the unicorn had a theme song it would probably be *'They'll never take me alive'* by Spear of Destiny, as this was the classical view of the unicorn. In Book 25 of *Indica* written by the Greek physician Ctesias in 398 BCE, he wrote of the unicorn that, *"You cannot catch them alive. The flesh of this animal is so bitter that it is inedible; it is hunted for its horn and ankle bone."* Ctesias went on to write about the virtues of the horn and its ability to protect against poisons and sickness. About a century later the Greek official Megasthenes wrote in *India* about the unicorn, and was the first person to mention the spiral rings on the horn. The unicorn had now become ribbed for extra pleasure! Of course on a more sensible level, it could be that he saw a narwhale tusk and the connection was made.

Pliny the Elder introduced the name *monoceros* (*'one horn'*) for the unicorn in his writings. The single horn subsequently became the horn of faith, and the unicorn was associated with Jesus. This effectively began with Tertullian of Carthage (c.160-220 CE), and continued with other major Christian writers such as Basileus (c. 330-379 CE) and Ambrose of Milan (340-397 CE). The latter enabled the unicorn and Jesus to predate Adam and be in the Garden of Eden, conveniently solving a knotty little theological issue about Jesus predating mankind at the same time. He wrote, *"Who is this unicorn but God's only son? The only word of God who has been close to God from the beginning! The word, whose horn shall cast down and raise up the nations?"* Here we can see where the virgin comes from. The horn of power represents Christ's power, and the virgin whose lap he bows his head in represents his mother Mary, who bore him in her own belly for nine months.

It was another Christian writer who introduced another magickal concept which hints at the divinity of the unicorn. Abbess Hildegard of Bingen (1098-1179) wrote in her book *Physica* that there was a little piece of metal or glass at the base of the unicorn horn, found when it was chopped off, in which a man would see his own face. This would turn into the Lapis Monoceros or unicorn stone of the alchemists, which was seen as being equivalent to the Philosopher's Stone. Obviously a creature possessing a stone which could cure all illnesses and bestow immortality must itself partake of a divine nature.

Young woman with Unicorn, sketch by Leonardo DaVinci,, circa 1480

In the Renaissance the unicorn was linked with the virgin goddesses in Italy. When Duke Borso d'Este had a series of planetary god murals painted in 1470, he had two unicorns pulling the chariot of the goddess Pallas Athene, to indicate her virgin nature. Shortly after this in 1499 the book *The Dream of Polophilo* contained a woodcut showing the goddess Diana in a chariot pulled by six unicorns. In a twist on this, the wild side of the unicorn was emphasised by the German artist Albrecht Durer (1471-1528) in his 1516 engraving *The Rape of Persephone,* which shows Hades abducting Persephone on the back of a unicorn rather than in a chariot.

So the unicorn undoubtedly has a divine nature, though how it is depicted has depended on the culture of the time. It is a sad reflection of the state of the world that today the unicorn is as likely to be shown as a cute fluffy house with pink tail and mane as it is a master of the wild. Still like all creatures of myth and spirit, it is a case of looking beneath the surface and finding the real essence – the divinity within the horn of the unicorn.

Bibliography
Charbonneau-Lassay, Louis; *The Bestiary of Christ*; 1992; Penguin; London
Godwin, Joscelyn; *The Pagan Dream of the Renaissance*; 2005; Weiser Books; Maine
Gotfredsen, Lise; *The Unicorn*; 1999; The Harvill Press; London
James, King (trans); *The Holy Bible*
White, T.H.; *The Bestiary: A Book of Beasts*; 1960; Capricorn; New York

STAG & UNICORN

**HEAR WITHOUT TERROR
THAT IN THE FOREST ARE HIDDEN
A DEER AND AN UNICORN.**

In the Body there is Soul and Spirit.

*"The Sages say truly
That two animals are in this forest:
One glorious, beautiful, and swift,
A great and strong deer;
The other an unicorn.
They are concealed in the forest,
But happy shall that man be called
Who shall snare and capture them."*

Extract from the *Book of Lambspring, a noble ancient philosopher, Concerning the Philosophical Stone; Rendered into latin verse by Nicholas Barnaud Delphinas,* Doctor of Medicine, a zealous student of this art.

Wild Hunt:

Rites & Experiences

© F.W.P. - Fotolia.com

HORN AT DAWN
By Rhys Chisnall

There is something that is just plain wrong about being up and about at four o'clock on a mid October Sunday morning. Surely this is a time better suited to going to bed after a great Saturday night out. However, here I was loading up my car with scuba diving gear and ready to head off on a detour for one of my yearly traditions. Later that day I was planning to head up to the North Norfolk coast where I was taking part in a Seasearch Marine life survey of two World War I wrecks for the Norfolk Wildlife Trust. First though I had an appointment to keep and had arranged to meet up with a friend and a trainee in the Craft to fulfil one of my yearly autumn traditions ready for the changing tides at Halloween; a meeting with the Dark Lord, the Horned God.

It was only a short car's journey of about twenty minutes or so along the dark misty country lanes to Helmingham Hall, which is located not too far to the North of Ipswich in the gently rolling Suffolk Countryside. I had arranged to meet Josey at the small Church that use to service the estate but now serves as an irregular parish church for an almost non existent congregation.

I pulled into the small church car park and despite it still being dark realised that I was the first one to arrive. My car headlights illuminated the mist, and then faded to darkness as I cut the engine and got out of the car into the cool damp autumn air. The leaves were still on the trees but were beginning to turn into their autumn hues of red and yellow, something that while I find beautiful, I also find sometimes sad and melancholy. The year was waning, its potential had been reached, the harvest, my harvest had been brought in and there was the long dark of the winter to look forward to. The tide was turning in the inevitable rhythm of the year. However, nature was also in her final bloom, the hedges rows that crowed the small church car park, were full of haws and blackberries. The Blackthorn on the other side of the road were heavy with sloes and the roses in the churchyard thick with rosehips, making me think of rosehip wine for the following year.

I cast an eye out towards the estate. It was down a slight incline that ran along an old path towards two distant lakes. No doubt fishing lakes left over from when the hall and park were in their heyday, before they were open to the public. Now they were untended and clogged with weed and rotting leaves. However, while I knew where they were they were they were all but obscured though by a heavy mist that hung in shrouds above the wet grass.

I didn't have to wait long before the laboured sound of a car engine and the hazy beams of headlights broke the silence of the dawn. My friend had arrived, pulling into the car park and waving with a cheerful grin. I waved back as she opened the door with a greeting and an offer of a hot and much needed cup of coffee.

Already the first hint of insipid light was creeping above the horizon and so after downing our coffees we headed across the still graveyard toward the little turn gate in the churchyard wall. The churchyard stood above the level of the mist, wreathed in gnarled old yews crowded with red berries. They were meant to keep

Witches away, I remember commenting with smile. There were no new graves here, nothing later than the nineteen sixties. And although the lawn of the churchyard was cut, some of the graves had been overtaken by brambles or covered in dog roses.

We went through the turn gate and entered the parkland of the Helmingham Hall estate. We could see the roof of the Elizabethan Hall pointing up above the mist as we followed the damp avenue down into the fog. It seemed as if it was wreathing about us, the air silent and windless and still. To our left and our right were the two fishing lakes, and our presence must have startled a sleeping mallard which shattered the silence with its raucous cry that sounds to me like mocking laughter.

It was then they we got the first sight of what we came to see. Through the mist, staring at us, perhaps thirty yards away was a young red deer stag. Not many tines yet on his antlers, and all alone, away from the hinds. He peered at us through the mist.

The red deer, Cervus elaphus is the UK's largest land mammal and along with the roe also is one of the two species of native deer. It is also one of the earliest creatures depicted in European human art with examples of cave painting in Russia dating back to the Palaeolithic some 40,000 years ago. In the autumn months the stags, pumped up on testosterone compete for the breeding rights over the hinds, and this rut is what we were here to see.

The beast peered at us, poised ready to flee, its nose in the air as it faced us. We in our turn froze to spot, silent not wishing to scare it. The air was windless, so I had no idea whether we were up or down wind of the creature. It was then, in that moment that it happened, echoing through the mist, renting the air, the throaty primal roar of a full grown stag, that sent the our youngster to flight. It turned tail and sprang, its muscles rippling, as it pranced with an easy grace away until the mist quickly swallowed it up.

The stag roared again. It is a sound that has echoed through Europe since before the dawn of history. Ancient, old, timeless in years beyond reckoning; it has echoed out when ice sheets covered most of Britain, when Neanderthal man competed with Homo sapiens in the hunt. It is primal, something forged within our DNA that makes the hairs on the back of our necks stand on end, the visceral roar of life and death itself. It tells of sexuality, lust and bubbling violence, both in nature, red in tooth and claw, and within ourselves. It is the very voice of the Horned One himself. I could feel the power coursing through my blood, as one after another the stags all about us in the park began a chorus of roars. It was the poetry of the voice of the Old One, echoing through the mouths of the lusty beasts. The roar, a boast that says I am the King, a way of avoiding direct violence, a ritual of power, status and survival.

Josey and myself crept forward deeper in the park towards the roaring stags. Occasionally, through the mist sheltering beneath trees, we would spy a group of shy fallow deer, which would then melt away as we approached, and then occasionally we would see a group of red hinds. The roaring grew louder and more frequent as the sun ascended higher into the sky, the mist was still thick. It would be several hours before the sun would burn it off.

Then a little way off we spied him, the monarch, his head held high as he bellowed his deep throaty roar. His head was crowned in many tined antlers; the velvet of the summer had been rubbed off, exposing the hard surface beneath. His crown, and also his weapons with which he would crash headlong into ritualised violence with others of his kind.

He as are we all, was part of the rhythm of life, the rhythm of the year, he would lose his antlers and he would lay down his crown to a younger fitter stag and eventually his life to old age. But his seed would endure from one King to the next, one generation to the next.

So it is with him, so it is with the rest of us. The Horned God dwells within us all, in the shadows behind the bright light of consciousness within the ebb and flows of our life, its patterns and rhythms, primal and dark. The God of sexuality, lust, death and change, for all life involves change, the alchemy of transformation. The change and alchemy of the mysteries, from birth and dependence to power, to the change of sex and sexuality, to the change of old age and the mystery of death. The Horned Lord is within us all as he was within those stags and within that park and within the whole of Nature.

The stag eventually moved off, and as the sun came up we climbed to the top of small rise, a vantage point where we saw many stags that morning. We even saw from afar the crashing together of antlers in the age-old ritual combat, but we didn't see another great stag up so close again. So the sun climbed, and the roars of the stags began to fall silent as the serious business of breakfast, both for the deer and us began to loom. We turned about and returned back through the churchyard and to our cars.

Two weeks later it was Halloween and I was at Coven for the Sabbat. The stang had been raised and candle light danced upon the naked bodies of the Witches. The air was heady with power as the Horned One the Dark Lord was invoked. The horned crown was placed upon the head of the High Priest by the High Priestess and in my mind I was taken back to the rutting of the stags, that primal ritual that echoes down through the ages and I felt the power rising within me. The same coursing in my blood, the same mysteries of life and death red in tooth and claw, yet still poetic, terrible and beautiful. Then the High Priest stood overshadowed, with the same power and the same primal mystery of that misty dawn he said.

"I am the God that waits….."

THE SONG OF AMERGIN

I am a stag: of seven tines,
I am a flood: across a plain,
I am a wind: on a deep lake,
I am a tear: the Sun lets fall,
I am a hawk: above the cliff,
I am a thorn: beneath the nail,
I am a wonder: among flowers,
I am a wizard: who but I
Sets the cool head aflame with smoke?

I am a spear: that roars for blood,
I am a salmon: in a pool,
I am a lure: from paradise,
I am a hill: where poets walk,
I am a boar: ruthless and red,
I am a breaker: threatening doom,
I am a tide: that drags to death,
I am an infant: who but I
Peeps from the unhewn dolmen, arch?

I am the womb: of every holt,
I am the blaze: on every hill,
I am the queen: of every hive,
I am the shield: for every head,
I am the tomb: of every hope.

The Song of Amergin, from *The White Goddess,* by Robert Graves

LIGHT IN THE EARTH

By John Canard

I know for many people the horned god is lord of the wild beasts, but I work with him in a different role. For me he is the lord of the wild places and their plants, as well as the nature spirits that dwell in them, the Green Man peering from the foliage. I have also found over the years that he works extremely well with Hekate, for reasons I do not pretend to guess.

Much of my method of working has been intuitive, using what feels right. This is not to say that I have ignored what I have learned from my teachers over the years, but sometimes you get an idea and have to run with it. A case in point - many years ago I was given a deer skin. Initially I decided to use it in ceremonies, with a horned helmet I had made, but then another idea struck me. Why not use it to represent all the places where I gather plants. Since then I have used the reverse of it as a map, painting a stylised map of my area, with different power plants marking the woods, fields and streams where I gather them. This has the added benefit that when I do wear the skin for ceremonies I am literally immersing myself in my sacred landscape!

I turn to the horned god when I need inspiration about herbs. Some years back I was trying to work out what the 'Black-Luggie' was in the rowan and red thread charm. I had come across suggestions it was the Jew's-Ear fungus, but was not convinced. The charm goes:

> *Black-luggie, lammer bead,*
> *Rowan-tree, and red thread*
> *Put the warlocks to their speed!*

Lammer bead is an old Scottish name for amber, so this obviously indicated tying an amber bead into the red thread you use to tie the two rowan twigs together in their equal-armed cross shape. But was there another ingredient to complete the charm? I had also read that some people speculated that 'Black-Luggie' was blackthorn, but I was not convinced. So I went to my grove of power to sit under a rowan tree and ask the one being I thought would know.

After calling to the horned god, I sat meditating under the tree and waiting for his answer. And when he answered me I got a surprise! The gist of his answer was *"It's me you idiot!"* That was all I got, so I knew I needed to do some research to find out what the horned god meant. The answer was quickly apparent. 'Luggie' is an old name for Lugh, so 'black-luggie' is literally black Lugh, or the light in the earth. And who is the light in the earth - the horned god! In other words you are calling on the horned god to bless your charm when you make it.

When I am looking for a herb that I haven't yet located in my area, I use my deer skin. I wrap myself in it and put on my horns, and meditate, asking the horned lord to guide me. Then I go on a journey, casting my mind through the fields and woods, looking for a sign in the landscape. Sometimes I see an animal, or a sparkle like a crystal catching the sunlight. Once I have received a sign of this kind, I thank the horned lord, gather my herb collecting kit and offerings and head straight for the locale. For me this is a modern version of *"dreaming the hunt"*, and it always guides me to the herb I am looking for, if it is to be found locally.

If I don't see any sign, I do a second version of this practice, where I ask the horned lord to guide me as part of his hunt, and I travel forth as one of his hounds, coursing across the landscape like a greyhound, but hunting for herbs rather than hares. This practice can be very tiring though if there is a great distance to travel, so I will often leave it until the next day to go looking for the place where I saw the sign. I drive to the locale rather than going on horseback, stopping somewhere convenient and making the final approach on foot, so I can do it in an appropriate manner to the nature of the herb.

There is always a price to be paid for magickal assistance, and in my case it is to spread the plants I have gathered. This means that on occasion I go on field trips, driving around the country and planting herbs with the intention of spreading them and encouraging their survival. I don't usually go back to the same place twice, not even to check, unless I get a sign through dream or vision to do so. Once I have seeded an area or left a cutting, my job is done and I prefer to minimize my impact on an area beyond contributing to the flora (or gathering it).

I have heard some magicians suggest that native psychedelics can contribute to your understanding of the plants in an area, but personally I prefer to reserve the use of such plants for particular times and places. If I want to open a fairy gate or commune with the dead then maybe I will, but in my experience the use of such plants is far too often an excuse to get *"wasted"* rather than do anything positive or magickal. For myself, in my relationship with the horned god, I do not use psychedelics, finding them unnecessary – it is not a connection that needs any enhancement of the senses!

One result of working with the horned god in this manner is that trees end up taking quite a bit of my time. It can be very hard to go past an oak tree without paying my respects, or singing to the hawthorn. Fortunately I have a very understanding partner, who knows where to look for me if I am not in shouting range. I dare say many people would find my behaviour somewhat eccentric if they were to come across me in my natural environment. However, they wouldn't of course, as I would blend in and wait for them to pass before getting on with whatever had taken me to the spot. If there is one lesson the horned god teaches you about being with plants, it is patience, and knowing when is the right moment to act. Don't think that plants are all about being slow, they have their own speed, it just isn't obvious until you become part of their world and wear the leaves on your face. When you can do that, then the horned god has truly accepted you into his kingdom.

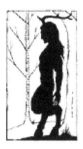

THE HORNED ONE RISES

By Peter J. Jaynes

Out of the Spirals....

Far from being an unknown god to our ancestors, Cernunnos was well known to those with an interest in ancient religion and archaeology for many hundreds of years before the rise of his popularity at the hands of Margaret Murray in the early part of the twentieth century and the later priesthood of the Wicca who would arise from within post-war Britain in the 1950's. Cernunnos is the name given to the horned god of the Gauls, whose name was found on an altar inscription dated to around two thousand years ago and which reads *"Ernunno"*. Though in the modern pagan revival Cernunnos is more often shown with antlers, the only depiction linked to his name clearly shows him with the horns of a bull! Cernunnos then clearly is not the stag horned god of the famous Gundestrup cauldron, but an entirely different deity.

As his name simply means *"horned one"* it is easy to see how the term *"Cernunnos"* could become linked to other horned deities through time. Indeed it would seem that variants of his name have shown up in various places over the years including Italy, which is something highlighted in the book *The Isles of the Many Gods* by

Rankine and d'Este. This is interesting as Cernunnos is often worshipped alongside the Italian demi-goddess Aradia by modern followers of the Wiccan tradition. An apparent conflict of pantheons then becomes less so, when a history of association with the same geographical area is taken into account.

Out of the Mist...

Like many who have discovered modern pagan spirituality, I felt empowered by the knowledge and techniques I found in books. I taught myself simple spell crafting techniques and also how to perform simple celebrations for the wheel of the year. I invoked the old gods and called on the power of the four elements to bless and protect me during my rites. As I grew in knowledge and experience I increasingly faced a problem which tore at my sensibilities on a regular basis. I could not reconcile my quest for knowledge with my quest for a spiritual and balanced life. The theologies put forward by many of the pagan authors seemed lacking to me and at the best reflected poor scholarship, so I probed deeper into the mysteries and history of this amazing god whose image dominates modern paganism as the archetypal masculine deity. I have discovered that there were many bull horned deities in England and Scotland, but that many of them have never been named. Instead these are the nameless horned gods of the history of the green isles, who might well have been Cernunnos. I visited the UK as part of my journey of discovery and found that the power flowed freely at some of the ancient sites I visited and did meditations and rituals at.

At one of these sites I met a priestess who facilitated meetings for me with a number of other people who would further help and inspire me with my work. At Midsummer that year I visited the ancient isle of Avalon, Glastonbury in Somerset. Out of the early morning mist rose the Tor into the morning sunshine, calling me to its summit. I journeyed up the spiral path round the Tor towards the zenith where the tower of St Michael stands, a strangely phallic monument of a masculine religious tradition, standing towering over the landscape.

I spent some time in meditation at the summit, contemplating my search for clarity on the conflicts I have been faced with whilst searching for the Horned God called Cernunnos. With the rising sun growing in power, the mists cleared from the landscape below, I realised for the first time that it was not the name which held the power, but the image of the man with the horns of power, the horns of a bull – one of the most powerful of the ancient Celtic animals and a very important one at that. To the Celts a bull represented power, strength and supremacy. The bull is often simply referred to as *"the beast"* in texts. The horns of the bull represent the power of that animal, which in itself was considered divine by the peoples of a wide variety of nations throughout human history.

Thus a man with the horns of a bull, would signify that power. The strength of a bull, held by a man would make a man supernatural, a god personifying power, strength and tremendous size. A virile and physically powerful man who could fight and protect his people, whilst ensuring plentiful offspring and the survival of the tribe. Cernunnos, the Horned One, is such a man-god.

Out of the House of Death...

Whilst all my conclusions clearly pointed towards a god who was a god of life and love, a god of fertility and joyfulness there was the other side of the view held by those of the Craft – Cernunnos as the God of the Underworld. Why would a god of strength be a god of the underworld associated with death? I pondered this question as I visited West Kennett Long Barrow in Wiltshire, near the ancient stone monument of Avebury just a few days later. I took my shoes off as I approached the monument and entered into it just as the

Sun was setting in the West behind me. With the intention of spending the night there I had come prepared and spent some time unpacking my tools and supplies and organising myself. Then I sat on the top of this ancient barrow and watched the last bits of the golden light of the Sun disappear in the horizon and caught the first glimpse of the rising Moon. Having celebrated the Midsummer Solstice a few days earlier, I was very aware of the fact that the power of the Sun, a powerful masculine symbol, was now on the wane, until its symbolic death and resurrection six months later at the Winter Solstice.

I entered the chamber at the back of West Kennett by walking down the narrow corridor and making offerings of specially prepared incense into each of the chambers, chanting and asking for the blessings of those who were interred there many thousands of years ago and the spirits of those who erected this monument for them. West Kennet was build around 3700 BCE and is one of the biggest barrows in the UK. Inside there are five sarsen stone chambers and when it was excavated 42 burials were found there, probably from the same family or tribe. With all that history I knew I had made the right choice when I chose this as a site for me to connect with Cernunnos as the Lord of Death. I invoked him using the traditional witch chant, often used in my coven at Samhain, the festival of death:

"Out of the spirals, out of the mist,
Out of the house of death, the Horned One rises…
Out of sleep, out of stone, out of the womb,
The Horned One rises,
He cometh to lead the Hunt, he cometh to lead the Dance…"

How appropriate! The barrow provided a womb like structure for me to be in, it was stone and it was a place of sleep for all the many who were buried there for thousands of years before their bodies were excavated, yet their spirits remained within, watching over me!

Slowly I felt the energy rising from above the barrow, descending to within. Of course the Horned One would not be a god of death at this time of the year; instead he lived without in the land, the corn fields which surrounded us green with the promise of a good harvest to come and in the forests and glades. And then I realized that he was the seed. Just like Saturn, the Roman god of time taught the people how to grow their own food, rather than having to rely on gathering from the wild alone, the Horned God and the seed were one. In the cold winter months the seed lies dormant within the womb of the Earth Goddess, by choice and by design, but with the warmth of the Sun it comes to life and rises from the Earth to become the green growth upon the Earth. The Horned God is the rising sap, without the Goddess he cannot be, but likewise, without the warmth of the Sun he cannot come into being.

The Horned One Rises...

As I sat I felt the power rising within me. The familiar feeling which I associate most with rituals of Drawing Down, in which the power of a deity is called down into a Priest or Priestess during ceremonies. The priest/ess then becomes a vessel for the manifestation of that deity for the duration of the ceremony, and may deliver a charge of words representing the wishes of the deity. I felt the warmth of the Horned God as my entire body tingled and felt the glow of his power, a solar power which instead of shining brightly glowed with a darkness I had not experienced before. Maybe that was because being a native of a big city in the modern world, I had never had the opportunity to perform such a rite in a burial chamber, let alone one with such an ancient history! I remembered the myths of the hounds of the underworld in Celtic mythology who accompanied the Horned rider at Samhain, I remembered that in just a few weeks the Horned God would be sacrificed as *"John Barleycorn"* to provide food and sustenance for the cold winter months and the base for beer and ale, which would sustain and warm many.

The Horned One rises each year from the darkness of the underworld, where he watches over the wealth within the Earth. The minerals such as gold, but also the most important wealth available to us, the seed, which contains within it not only the promise of what is to come, but also the promise of continued life. Without the seed, there would be no food for sustenance, and through providing the seed, the Horned God also provides for us and ensures that life upon the Earth continues.

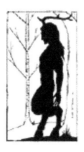

MY BEARDED MAN

By Thea Faye

I cannot say when I first became aware of the Horned God, because He's always been in my life, in one guise or another. His appearance has gradually changed over the years, but He has always been essentially the same and usually I refer to him as My Bearded Man, because that's exactly what He is – a man with a beard who looks out for me. However, He has named himself otherwise – Cernunnos.

Now at heart, I'm a sceptic. I don't take anyone's word for anything, especially not when they are an Otherworldly entity who could have a very different agenda to what they present. And I'm also not so egotistical as to assume that a God would want to take time out from His busy schedule to hang out with me. So even now, after many, many years of a close relationship, there is a part of me that sees him as a Cernunnos, rather than necessarily the Cernunnos. But as far as our relationship is concerned, my slight reservations don't seem to bother Him too much.

Now many encounters with the Horned One often veer off into the realms of pornography, which is hardly surprising, and there have been a fair few Beltanes when, as soon as He arrived, the air was charged with an eroticism so thick that no foreplay was necessary and all it took was a look and I was His. Happy times indeed. But my favourite memory of my bearded man is much softer, gentler, tender, enjoyable as those other occasions may have been.

In 2005, shortly after a major magickal event, as is often the way, a big life change came up. My husband and children all have dual nationality, so when the opportunity arose to emigrate, we were able to jump at it with no hesitation. It was to prove to be the most stressful time of our lives. We had the thought that we might like to go in July; a job opening came up in August; my husband was on the other side of the planet in September, leaving me behind with our two children, aged 1 and 2, a house to sell and visas and passports to arrange, not to mention arranging residency for me, the lone non-citizen of our new home. It was the beginning of a two and a half month separation, an experience I hope never to repeat, especially since we had no idea how long it would last.

If you have not been through an emigration, you cannot imagine the upheaval it causes and the amount of preparation required, especially when you have to do it alone because your partner has had to go ahead to pave the way. The children's passports caused more problems than I could have thought when my younger child point blank refused to co-operate with the photographer, necessitating no fewer than three trips, the last involving the shop being kept open just for us, just to have a shot that looked vaguely like her, only for it to be my son's photo that was rejected because his hair was too long. I had medicals and police checks to arrange, animals to rehome or get export ready and the selling of the house... Well, suffice to say that it is possible to have your house spotless and ready to view when you have two toddlers, but it really takes it out of you.

There were times when I thought I would explode with the pressure of it all.

But through it all, He was there. He held my hand when I needed, stroked my hair to calm me and showed me what our new home would look like. During this time, His appearance went through another one of its transformations, this time, appearing to me with a lion's head, although, as always, He was still the same Cernunnos. He offered me support and knew exactly what I needed to help me through. Many nights when I was too wound up to sleep, I found myself walking along a beach with Him, the sand black, something I'd never seen before. We would talk about everything that was happening before sitting down to watch the waves crashing against the strand and I would lean against Him, His arm around me to keep me safe as I finally was able to relax enough to drift off to oblivion.

We found a buyer, which was luckier than we could have imagined since a couple of days after I left the country, the oil depot a mile up the road from where we lived exploded. It could have caused our sale to fall through, at a time when we were able to do nothing about it because we were no longer in the country, but the buyers were staying with relatives in the town at the time so knew that it hadn't damaged the house. The Gods were certainly smiling on us – but talk about a sign that you had done the right thing in leaving!

My husband and I were reunited and he took time off work to show us the local sites. He drove us to a local beach and of course, it had black sand. And the name of the landmark the beach was known for?

Lion's Rock.

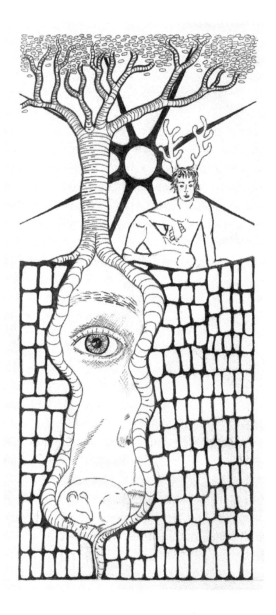

A SMALL MOUSE
By Magin

I looked for him by his lady's side,
but she was riding her chariot high
And only whispered with a soft smile
That he loved her silver light,
but dwelt upon and within the Earth.

I looked for him through the candlelight
and the dancing incense smoke
But their natures were too contained,
too restricted for his immense spirit.

I looked for him in the meadow, and thought I caught a glimpse of
something, someone
Glinting in the sunlight, rustling through the grasses –
But it was probably the wind.

I looked for him on the high hill of the ancestors and in the hushed twilight
I thought I saw something, someone,
Comforting the crumbling stones –
But it was probably just the living.

I looked for him in the forest
and thought I heard the hunting call
And saw his horns, immense and terrible –
But it was probably just my fear trembling in the darkness.

I retreated to my garden and sat beneath my own fruit tree
Beside me, a smiling stranger bade me rest a while before continuing my
search,
For whosoever, whatever, it was I needed.

He played the flute to me
His great horns spread out above us, bathed in light
His song was of the dancing sunlight,
a heartfelt prayer by candlelight,
Of the playful wind and the cold realm of the dead
Of the beating hearts of the living and of the great Wild Hunt
Of the need for both fear
and courage in the hearts of all creatures.
His song was of peace and sorrow, joy and pain, hope and loss.
It was of himself.

With his song in my heart I will begin my search once more.

My relationship and the way I work with the Horned God is different to the ways I have encountered other deities. He is elusive and yet as present and tangible as my own heart; he is permeable and multi-faceted but also rooted and singular. I have not, as is my practice with most deities I work with, carefully researched his nature, correspondences and realms – for I have found that in doing so I only find out about one aspect, maybe a different deity entirely, and my own Horned God fades out, back into the shadows. I do work with him in his various aspects but this piece is not about that, it is about my own, special relationship with him which, I believe, is as unique as his relationship with every other creature and being in his vast realm.

I have a similar working relationship with the generic *'Lunar Goddess'*, but there is a significant difference. Back when my religion of birth had ceased to have meaning for me she emerged as the Moon from behind a cloud, present and all embracing. I didn't even have to express a need; it was just like a veil falling away. I worked with her for many years; as I learnt more her consort appeared as a void, an absence. The Lord of the Wilds, it seemed, had no wish to reveal himself to me and I, in my turn, shied away from dark places, preferring the reassuring light of the Lady (*'Reassuring'*? You might ask - naïve of me I know).

I enjoy painting and one birthday a friend presented me with two wooden figurines (think peg doll but more stylish). I set about painting my goddess immediately but put the god aside so I could ruminate on how to make his horns. Time passed and my tranquil lunar goddess sat upon her altar with an unpainted, unshaped *'god'* beside her. They accompanied me on all my travels from home to home, place to place and still the Horned One and I kept our distance.

I progressed on my path until it became clear to me that I couldn't put off the meeting if I wished to proceed further. As I had discovered more complexity within my own practice and more deities in their myriad aspects, my Lunar Goddess had changed - no longer the placid and nurturing Lady of the Moon, she had become so much more. When I set out my altar with my Lord and Lady upon it she seemed to hold back and I knew that I was lost once more and this time she wouldn't seek me out. I went out and bought materials for the horns of my figurine and resumed my (previously half hearted) quest for the Horned God. Many walks, songs, meditations and hours spent staring into space and I had not progressed much further.

This was the point in my life where everything went a bit wrong. My life, for want of a better description, grew steadily smaller. I was very ill and couldn't do very much at all; it also became clear that some of the things I had relied upon were not what they seemed. Unable to go out or do much for myself I focused on the things I could do and, without any other options presenting, finally began to paint. As I painted I realised why I had avoided the journey for so long and not really committed to the path throughout my recent work. To me the Horned God was frightening, wild and unpredictable, a natural force. I felt intimidated and threatened; the God represented a test I could not prepare for and as such, might actually fail. Bearing in mind, however, that I could no longer work, couldn't move all that much and was about to lose my home, there didn't seem much more that I could fail in really. So, armed with my ritual equipment, goddess figurine and newly painted and be-horned God I descended to the garden (with much swearing as going down stairs on crutches carrying ritual equipment is not easy) and in the smallest outdoor space I have ever worked in I asked the Horned God to bring his blessings into my life and finally set my completed figurine beside his lady.

The ritual itself was peaceful. The sun was out and I was so happy to have made it out of the grotty house. The Horned God did not present himself in the roaring and terrible aspect I had dreaded, he was gentle and kind. In his hand he held a small mouse, curled up and asleep. During all the images shown to me and as the animals of the wild wood presented themselves, the mouse did not stir once. At the end of the ritual I felt rested and more myself somehow.

I have not experienced many *'dark nights of the soul'* but that night was one of them. I was in pain, I felt unsafe and alone, far away from those who cared for me and far too close to those who didn't. As I lay awake in the darkness the tangible presence of the Horned God began to stir around me and the moment I had been dreading occurred as he rushed forth, towering and menacing above me. I cannot begin to describe to you the power and the rage that I felt around me, the sheer animal force of this mighty being is unlike any other I have ever felt. Above me and around me he roared and I, like the mouse, curled up, safe, secure and loved by this storm of rage; the emotional and physical pain that had engulfed me fled before his terrible gaze and I fell asleep. The rage of the Horned God is mighty indeed, but the love and blessings he bestows are greater still.

ENCOUNTERS IN THE WOODS
By Harry Barron

I would like to tell you a story of events that happened to me a long time ago as a boy, when the Horned God introduced Himself to me for the first time, even though I did not at that time recognise Him and I had no idea that Wicca, Earth-based spiritualities or suchlike even existed. I identify with many creatures in the wild around me: the proud Horse, being the Sign I was born under in the Chinese Zodiac; the noble Swan, associated with one of my given names; the wise Salmon, who appeared to me once in a vision quest and is coincidentally on the emblem of the town I was born in but it is the majestic Stag I identify with more intimately than with any of the other animal guides, not just because he represents the embodiment of the God for me, but also because the Stag has appeared to me in person more times than any other creature. This is how the story goes...

As a pre-teen child, I had a very real fear of being alone in the woods. Any woods, anywhere, but in particular, the woods in the village where I grew up South Wales. I had heard stories of bogeymen from other children at the school and church I attended and of course, I was terrified of being caught by these malevolent beings and never seen again – despite the fact that no child had ever disappeared in the village. As for the forests nearby (and living in Wales, even South Wales, they were never far away!) there was no way I would even go anywhere near them alone... I had read Tolkien's tales of *The Hobbit* and I knew what lurked in them!

At 7 years of age, I joined the Cub Scouts in the village, whose hut was on the edge of those woods and we often went into them for our outdoor pursuits. We were taught how to recognise and identify plants and trees, we went on bivouacking adventures, played al fresco games, built treehouses and such like. In fact, when I was with other Cubs, the woods were my friend and looking back on it, I realise that it was all good preparation for a later life as a Wiccan. Even when we were playing hide and seek in the woods and I had been separated from the rest of the pack, I still felt secure, as I knew the other kids were somewhere in the woods along with Akela and Baloo, the grown-up leaders of the troop and to be honest, as I was not focusing on being alone, I did not think I was alone and being scared did not enter into my 7-10 year old head. Isn't it deliciously ironic, though, how the actual animals Akela and Baloo (along with Kaa), anthropomorphised characters from Kipling's *Jungle Book*, would have been two good reasons for me to have been fearful of going into the forest alone a millennia or so ago when bears and wolves (and snakes!) were common forest dwellers of the island of Great Britain?

This fear of being unaccompanied in the woods and especially being alone in the dark in the woods followed me into pubescence. Just before my 12th birthday, after the family had moved from South Wales to Southern England, I was sent to an all-boys boarding school somewhere in Sussex, a popular location for such schools. The focal point of this school was the Quadrangle, a square surrounded by school blocks, the Chapel, a huge hall where concerts and exams were held and the Dining Hall. The boarders lived in boarding houses in a long row of houses at equidistant locations on either side of the Dining Hall, where we all congregated three times a day to eat. Underneath the boarding houses ran a passage – a remnant from the war, where the boys would be sent down to escape the destruction the German Luftwaffe might rain upon the school and its occupants with their bombs during the Second World War. It was now mainly used for the plumbing and electrical works for the school, as well as having storage for suitcases and drying out wet clothes and it also acted as a passageway and refuge from heavy rain when we needed to get to the Dining Room dry. It was miserable eating wearing those wet, heavy, woollen coats!

Some of the older boys had nurtured cruel streaks, as older boys are wont to do and had created ghost stories, with which they used to gleefully taunt and scare the younger boys and one of the more gruesome tales I had heard featured this underground passageway and not only did I become afraid of being in the woods adjacent to the school and into which we were sent periodically for outdoor recreational activities, but I also became terrified of being in that passageway even when I was with a crowd of other boys and I would constantly look behind me nervously as I hurried along to the Dining Hall, lest the ghosts catch me, mutilate me and hang my decaying body up on the walls as a warning to the other pupils, as that particular story portrayed... There was no way I would ever be found in that passage alone, even to retrieve my suitcase to go home or to dry my damp clothes. It could rot there for all I cared and I was content walking around in wet socks! Those stories designed to terrorise the younger boys, well, they definitely worked!

Next to the school and considered part of its grounds lay some woodlands; the school was in the countryside, again a good place for an aspiring nature-lover and the smells from the school's dairy farm, which often permeated the local atmosphere and occasionally put everyone in the Infirmary with gastroenteritis, along with the scents of the flora and fauna from the hills and fields around us, were all part of our consciousness, embodied in lessons we had in our first year called Environmental Studies, an introduction to the natural sciences, which was really a posh name for studying nature, ecology and the effect it has on us and we on it. This Church of England School certainly knew how to educate Pagan Children well!

These woods were used not just by the Scout troop that was based at the school, but also by the various boarding houses for their physical exercises and outdoor games. I remember one yearly ritual at the start of the school year involved all new boys being thrown into the wood's pond fully dressed, in sports clothes, of course, with the full approval of the attendant Housemaster as part of their initiation into school life! Did I mention that most of the masters at the school were Freemasons? It was all supposed to be in good fun and supposedly good for the body and spirit and occasionally the Housemaster ended up in the drink along with his charges!

Those same nightmares of being alone in the woods (not to mention the passageway under the boarding houses!) came back to haunt me threefold.

One sport we were encouraged to take part in at least once a week was called a steeplechase which is a cross-country run that culminated in coursing through these ominous woods on the final lap before reaching the finish line back at the boarding house. Or in my case, I would gently meander through the green fields and saunter over the gently rolling hills before I would gather my energy and sprint through the woods as fast as I could so that I did not have to linger in there any longer than I needed to.

So what, you may ask, has any of this schoolboy story got to do with the Horned God?

I am getting there, I promise...

One day, when I was a little bit older and already in Senior House, while running through these very same woods during my bi-weekly steeplechase ritual, a sport that I actually loved and became quite good at, despite my dread of being in those woods by myself, I became aware of something rustling in the undergrowth. At this time of my life, I was going through a Christian phase (this was a Church of England school and Christianity was encouraged, although admittedly rather half-heartedly but I was a fervent member of the Christian Union) and I had already lost my belief in the bogeyman and also in the existence of Father Christmas, although inexplicably, I had not stopped believing in fairies, not really being sure if they were truly wicked, as Christianity would have us believe, mischievous, as various fairy tales recounted, or as benign elemental beings, as some new age writers were beginning to inform us; it was a contradiction that flew in the face of my Christian tenets and I knew it. So I simply ignored all hints of fairy activity that my nascent psychic senses were definitely picking up. Nevertheless, the rustling startled me and I remember clearly feeling my heart racing, thinking it that it must be some kind of malevolent entity coming out of the realms of darkness to capture my soul and whisk me off to some doleful and dismal hell to punish me for my belief in fairies and other suchlike heresies.

But instead of bolting, as I would typically have done, I stood still; I am not sure why and there, out of the scrub emerged a magnificent stag. Instead of being frightened, I was spellbound, too stunned to move, as I now believed that I was receiving blessings from the Jehovah/Jesus/Holy Ghost that I believed in at the time, in contrast to what I had believed just moments before, and this was a manifestation of His wonderful creation. We looked at each other for what seemed like an eternity – these encounters can be so magical that time seems to stand still and in fact I do not know how long we stood there looking at each other – but there was no fear and the stag was unperturbed by my presence. The sounds of other runners approaching us through the woods startled us both; the magnificent creature ran off back into the woods and I continued my course through the remainder of this stretch of the steeplechase, deep in thought and feeling blessed by what I had just been part of.

As you have just read, in those days, I was a Christian – I knew no better and this deep desire I felt to express my sense of spirituality manifested itself through Christian worship as it was easily accessible to me and so I embraced it wholeheartedly, although also uncomfortably, as even at that early age, I had precociously developed a deep-rooted belief in reincarnation, spirit guides and other heresies, which conflicted violently with the teachings of the evangelical, inflexible and immovable Church that I was a member of. It was to be years later that I realised that I had had an encounter with the Horned God, but even believing then that I had been blessed by God Jehovah, the encounter with the stag had worked a profound effect on me and from that day, I lost my fear of being in the woods alone and I was able to enjoy my preferred sport of steeplechasing. As for the passage under the school, sure, I was still terrified of that place until the day I left and no doubt my old suitcase has long since rotted and turned into dust!

Let me fast forward a few years and introduce you to my young adult life; I remember once having this inexplicable urge to go for a walk in a local forest near to where I was living in South West London – AT NIGHT. I felt the need to escape the city, its aggressive citizens and it seemed the logical thing to do. Having long moved to the cities of Portsmouth, Leeds, and now London, I had long forgotten my boyhood and adolescent country roots and I had also forgotten about my past fear of being in the woods alone...

until it was too late and I was already somewhere deep between the dark bodies of the trees looming above my head, their leaves rustling secretively to each other, that a stranger was in their midst and I was too far from the car park and civilisation to be able to bolt to safety in time. This was the first time I had ever been alone in the forest at night and I was beginning to feel very panicky indeed...

Before I carry on, I should tell you, that a few years previously in my early 20's, I had faced a crisis in my life that had not only threatened to engulf me, but also threatened to destroy me and this crisis had prompted me to do some spiritual searching as Christianity no longer held the answers I was looking for, nor did it offer me any comfort from the impending disaster. Needless to say, I survived that fateful episode with the minimum of fuss, but it was the spiritual changes in my consciousness that are important to this story. I had discovered the Goddess and abandoned God! Initially I had been drawn towards Taoism, which was a logical choice as I had been living and studying in China the previous year and I still hold Taoism dear to my heart, especially since these days, I am a practitioner of the Chinese Healing Arts; Taoism has become part of my essence. However, my studies in Taoism gradually pointed towards the Western Mystery Traditions, Paganism and more significantly, Wicca, which is another story in itself; but I came to Wicca reluctantly, kicking and screaming, still clutching onto my outdated and rigid Christian tenets from my previous spiritual life. I had clearly heard the call of the Goddess and I had no choice but to respond. What I had not yet realised is that I had already met *"The God"* (as opposed to *"God"*) in person all those years before as a teenager when I was at school; not Jehovah, that scarily vengeful and vindictive God but the mild and wild Horned God personified in this magnificent Stag, who had allayed my fear of the woods, its inhabitants and of Nature.

Having come out of a punishing patriarchal religious system, I was at first suspicious of any god-form and I believe, along with many others that this may be one of the reasons why the God is not as popular as the Goddess within Western Wiccan Devotionals. Which is a great tragedy.

But I am heading out on a tangent here and I'd like to get back to my story.

... so, there I was, in the middle of the forest, surrounded by all these nightly noises: hooting owls, flapping birds disturbed by my body brushing past the trees where they had made their nests, small animals scuttling off into the depths to avoid my footsteps; all noises that were increasing my panic and making me wish I had not given in to this mad notion of getting away from the city during the hours of darkness! What had I been thinking? This irrational fear that I had borne of the dark and of the imaginary and depraved denizens of the frightening forest was so menacing, that I was truly scared for my sanity, if not my life. But suddenly, I became aware of the presence of a herd of deer and some magnificent stags amongst them. Memories of my previous encounter all those years ago when I was at school came flooding back to me and the surging panic left me as quickly as it had overwhelmed me. This is when I realised that I had met The Horned God before and I felt that I was once more in the presence of the Horned God and that particular fear subdued and from that day forth, I never experienced dread of entering forests alone again, even at night, as I am always aware of that Divine presence watching over me, which is comforting.

But what is there really to fear in Nature in the British Isles? What could harm me? We no longer have any wolves or bears, although we still have snakes, which by and large keep a discrete distance from humankind. I no longer believed in bogeymen and I felt immune to the wiles of the fairy folk (something I would reconsider some years later, however!) so, I was in actual fact quite safe. I felt protected by the spirit of the Horned God and despite His feral and untamed nature, there is a gentleness surrounding Him and His mirth and mild amusement of my fear of Nature were perceptible.

As Wiccans, we tend to dress the Goddess in the clothes of the Natural World, forgetting that the Horned God is also an intrinsic part of that very same Nature. He is an inseparable part of us and as Wiccans, we can often overlook Him, forgetting that the God and Goddess are part of the Whole – Divinity united.

My third personal encounter with the Horned God occurred as I was working towards my first degree initiation into Wicca, as I had long since joined a group that was training me to become a fully functioning Wiccan Initiate. I was feverishly going through all my checklists of what I needed to do before I even dared approach my Elders and request initiation and I had been doing a great deal of devotional work to the Goddess, to the exclusion of the God.

One evening, I had been invited to a dinner party in Oxfordshire, not far from Blenheim Palace and I was driving along a darkened road along side that Palace, when suddenly, I turned a corner and there in the middle of the road, was a stag. It was all I could do to slam on the breaks not to hit the creature, which I had succeeded in doing; but the stag had already taken fright and rushed into the headlights of the car, causing a significant amount of damage before he bounded back into the woodlands surrounding the Palace. Startled and angrily inspecting the damage caused to the car, I continued on my way, anxious to put in an insurance claim the next day.

When I did put in the claim form for repairs to the car, having explained what had happened, the insurers came back stating that this had been *"an act of god"* and was not covered by the insurance policy and that I would have to sue to owners of Blenheim Palace (Queen Elizabeth II) if I wanted to seek compensation. Scandalous and dishonest, sure. But what struck me was the phrase *"act of god"*. It might well have read *"act of The God"* and I suddenly realised that I had all but forgotten the God and what He represented for me. This was a wake-up call for me. An expensive one, mind you but He needed to remind me that the Goddess is only part of the story and that I had been ignoring Him and this had been His way of getting back my attention and devotion.

If you look at the symbol that many people associate with Chinese philosophy, the symbol that is commonly referred to as the Yin Ying Symbol, you can see representation of the dualistic nature of the Divine, or the Universe: the masculine and the feminine aspects of Nature and the Universe, very similar to the way we represent the God and Goddess in Wicca. They are intertwined and inseparable, flowing into each other, which cannot be represented by a static diagram but it should be stressed they are ONE. One cannot function without the other and we as Wiccans have sometimes been guilty of ignoring the masculine in favour of the feminine, in the same way that monotheistic religions have been guilty of not only ignoring the feminine, but exorcising it completely from their theologies.

This was the message that the God was conveying to me after the encounter with the stag in the road.

In recent years, I have moved back to Wales, to the mountains and forests and this has partly been as a result of those early experiences meeting the Horned God in the Woods and Forests. I can no longer imagine living in a city now, as I feel not only the God, but also the Goddess in the soil, rocks, water and air of the open spaces; an experience a city-dweller could not really appreciate. Not that the cities and big towns are devoid of the Divine, but you have to look harder for them sometimes.

These days, I have no more fear of the dark, but I welcome it; nor do I fear being alone in the woods and forests – I often trek into them by myself and have even been known to camp out alone near the summit of forested mountain peaks. The feeling I now get from these places thrills me and I feel that much closer to the Masculine Divine and the awe and reverence I feel when I encounter any animal, especially stags and deer is perceptible and I give thanks to the God, as I can feel His spirit permeate my being. He has a strong presence in my house, as there are paintings of the Horned God and of The Stag in various locations and I not only see Him in the calls of the wildlife around me, but also hear Him in the wild winds howling past me and feel Him in the hot summer sun warming my exposed flesh in the garden and on the beach. He is the rawness of Nature, destructive in His might, but also gentle and protective towards His own. He is Cernunnos, Pan, Herne, Hu Gadarn, Puck; Lord of the Wild Woods.

It is my hope that my little anecdote will help you lose any apprehension you may have of Nature and to inspire you to go for a walk into your local woodlands and forests and meet the Horned God in person. He is there waiting for you, calling you; of that you can be sure. If you are suffering from pale skin from having spent too much time under the Moon with the Goddess recently, why not go and say hello to Him under the Sun. He might just surprise you with a little swim in a pond!

A QUEST FOR HORNS

By Stephen Blake

When I sat down to write about *"The Horned God"* I quickly realised two things: people's experiences of him vary more than with most deities, and it's also difficult to find a visual image of him that anyone agrees on. This could be because (depending on the tradition in question) he is a mix of so many figures - an exuberant personality of Pan-like wild joy and vitality, the dread Lord of death and the Underworld, the leader of the Wild Hunt, Gwyn Ap Nudd, an amalgam of the entire male side of Nature, the Lord of the trees and animals... He is the King, and consort, and shining child. Where on earth do we begin looking for *"The"* Horned God? My own history with him seems to be a constant search for this, so I decided to focus this contribution on it.

I was in my early twenties when I felt the time was right to pursue the pagan and magical paths which had always interested me. This wasn't an easy decision (my family would be against it if they found out, and *'the pagan Horned God'* was never going to be an easy one to explain.) So, knowing that it would cause trouble with my family and being well aware of the prejudice from employers and the public towards magical thinking (let alone any path that actually uses the word *'witch'*) I was cautious about entering into the religion. It was definitely what I wanted, but I didn't make a commitment until I'd found a group I trusted fully – I was very lucky in finding people to work with and joined an initiatory Wiccan coven.

During my time in the outer court there were exercises to explore how I felt about a general Horned God figure. Wicca does many things deliberately differently to the more well-known religions, and for men in particular identifying with the Horned God brings a set of associations that are out of favour in today's society (and wildly so with any Church). Fertility and the body are not frowned upon in Wicca as they are in other religions, and the God is primal: strong, passionate, joyful and vital. A Wiccan works directly with their Gods and is more like a Priest than a member of the congregation. I had some experience in shamanic traditions before entering paganism, and my first concern was with finding out more about the Horned God's attributes (not for any academic reason, but because I would be experiencing them intensely). Therefore, my first step was to find out where the boundaries of his personality lay... but I was going to have to do it in a heavily experiential way.

Male strength is not as popular a concept in today's society as it used to be. We don't have many roles for warriors in modern cities, and aggression is too often misused. I quickly found that the energy and determination which comes with the God's physical strength is not just destructive aggression, unnecessary or uncontrolled. It is wild and joyful, worthy of a mighty King. I knew about some similarly horned gods (Pan having goat horns, others with those of a Bull) but felt I needed to put a more detailed personality and motives to this one in order to better understand him. For example, he is often associated with Forests, and the horned and wild animals that live within them. I turned this around: if he is the spirit of the Forest, then does the forest tell us anything about him?? And much more to the point, what can it help us feel about him?

Books from many traditions say that he is the epitome of unstoppable might, present in the thrusting of green plants from the soil, the rage and passion of the hunt... but have you been in a forest recently? It's very quiet. Events within it do not always happen with great frequency or violence. If anything, it's very calm. Does this mean that one part of the Horned God is always this calm, or that there could be a separate aspect of Him that is?

I went to some woodland near London and sat, listening. Despite the tranquillity, there was strength in the meditative silence of the forest. It was the patient resilience of the Oak and the cloaked might of a powerful energy held in reserve. I felt a knowing watchfulness over everything in the domain. His magic there - rather than a sure Kingship over the Underworld, or the battle and lightning of the Wild Hunt - is the sunlight through leaves and slow mist of the forest. I felt him in the harmony and instinctive awareness of the creatures... and when sudden violence from a predator gained it a meal, he was there too. It was this presence which set him apart from other deities for me, because I felt it strongly even in urban surroundings. He is too integral to nature to be absent from any area, but his presence is strongest amongst the trees.

Now it's true that our modern experience of forests is different to even a few hundred years ago. The Woods can be a dark and dangerous place, and I'm not suggesting that this flavour of things should be ignored. Over time, I've felt the Horned God's presence in many different environments and learned new things from each, and I hope readers will do the same – subjective experience is what this book is all about!

Many of the God's aspects are linked with darkness: the more Germanic versions of the leader of the Wild Hunt have him riding through the night sky during storms, while other paths emphasise his role in death and the underworld. In contrast, his journey through the seasonal celebrations known as the Wiccan 'wheel of the year' is nearer that of the Sun.

So I looked at things from the opposite direction once again. Instead of saying that there are certain themes of the Sun linked to the Horned God, I attempted to take every role of the Sun and see what it would tell me about the God.

Now there's an obvious danger with doing this. The Sun has been linked with reason and science in ways that are the opposite of the powerful wild emotion that the Horned God can stir up (even before we consider his role as a God of Magic). His is a primal Kingship, not a connection to well-ordered civilisation or city society. So it was quite clear from the beginning that while the Horned God might embody some solar aspects such as health, vitality and male strength, this symbolism is not the whole story. The Sun can become a tool to force the world to be mundane, all its secrets revealed, the remainder purely measurable and scientific. As a Wiccan I find the idea of that kind of world terrifying – we are of the full Moon in the darkness as well as the summer Sun; we're never going to stop loving the magic, secrets and blessings of the Goddess that come with the night sky and our natures. Most male pagans know that rejecting half of themselves or the World is both futile and harmful. The Sun is the fire that powers our passion and magic just as much as the Moon does, and we should explore it in the spirit of that fiery joy.

After using some of the themes this way, I felt that I was starting to get a better idea of what the God was and wasn't. It may sound impossible to do this for a deity, but his relationship to the Sun felt very specific. Even excluding some aspects (as I did above for some of the more scientific solar influences) this still left lots of possibilities. As I took more steps into Wicca, I found myself paying attention to every part of nature I saw all through the day, and discovered more questions about the solar aspects - which part of him could be associated with The Dawn, for example?

I've always been drawn to Dawn Goddesses. Eos ruled the hours of dawn and the morning in the Greek pantheon (even when the Sun itself was male.) Many other cultures also saw this time as comforting, gentle and reassuring, not the attributes usually associated with most male Gods. There didn't seem to be anywhere in classical myth to find a male perspective that might help explore the Horned God's role at this time. More recently however, we have the stunning chapter from *The Wind in the Willows* entitled *'The Piper at the gates of Dawn'*. This describes an awesome and glorious Pan-like god arriving with the morning sun. It is easy to see the God at noon, particularly in heat of Summer when He is then at the fullness of his strength and beautiful might. The Dawn is trickier to define - I had to ask myself, is there any room in his personality for this gentler side too?

I don't think there needs to be. Sunlight penetrating darkness is not always gentle, it can be cruel and inevitable. It is certainly invincible, always winning the preliminary fight of pre-dawn before the flaming spear of the first rays explode over the horizon. At the famous site of New Grange in Ireland, where sunlight enters the long tunnel and illuminates the chamber on the Winter Solstice, it has been described as slicing into the darkness quickly and devastatingly – *"like a sword"* rather than a slow rosy glow. And anyway, choosing to be gentle does not imply weakness. The Horned God has wisdom, and it is certainly wisdom that lets a strong warrior choose to sheath his sword. A wild passion must still be controlled by the bearer, unless he is to be a danger to his allies as well. I had no problem with the God being close enough with the natural cycles to restrain his full might during the dawn.

And so, while getting up horribly early to commute to work, I saw the sunrise through the train window. And it was glorious. Here in the middle of winter when I was getting up in the dark, and the frost seemed to have the whole country in a determined grip, the strength and passion of the Sun flooded over the landscape like a shout. The sky was clear and cold, and no cloud stopped the incredibly pure light from breaking over everything. There are swans on the river next to the path I take to work, and I've always seen them and the slow body of water as a potent image of the Goddess. On that day more than ever, I felt the Sun as a male force sending its strength to turn the whole scene to gold, a reminder that he was still there in the middle of the dark and cold days. This was a fully pagan and male being, a majestic King whose antlers demonstrated his power to reach down into the earth and throw his will to the horizon.

I continued to explore how the Horned God and the Sun could be connected. I was coming to it through initiatory Wicca, but many traditions make the same link, particularly between the Horned Gods, the Oak Tree and the Sun. When I mentioned my ideas on Dawn to my High Priest, he said *"What about the eclipse?"* A magical time when the Moon blocks the solar sphere, imposing its own magic and mystery on the land during the day… the God and Goddess working together. What is the nature of the God at this time?

This was all very abstract, though. It was fine to explore other related themes (and Forests and the Sun, particularly linked to his role in the wheel of the year, have always been the two I've felt strongly) but there was one question that drove me to keep looking for more:

What is the *"usual"* image of the Horned God figure himself in the mind of the average pagan?

It is Harvest time, and the wheat is being brought in. This is the inescapable role of the God – to be cut down in his prime and then return to strength in the New Year. It has to happen. The roles are reversed too, of course. The Goddess often feels bigger, more immaterial and immortal than the man-shaped figure who can die, but there are plenty of legends that have it the other way. Persephone is the Summer when she goes down into the Underworld, disappearing for a time to return in Spring. The powerful, wise Lord of the Underworld is a much more constant deity than the cyclical dying harvest God.

But in my Wiccan celebrations this particular year, the Harvest is about the Corn King and no other. The fields are golden, the Summer is still with us. I have felt the Horned God in darkness, in candlelight – now Beltane is past and he has tasted life and is King.

We are in the fields. I wear a light circlet of twisted wheat. The other witches are smiling, overjoyed. Now is the time we see the earlier promise of fertility fulfilled in the land, the harvest is in. It has been difficult: this year there was a drought in Britain, and then heavy rains at the worst possible time before harvesting. I bind myself to that – no bananas from Mexico, apples from South Africa. We rise and fall as the land does, and I will not ignore the current state of things. I will not reach out effortlessly for fruit from the other side of the World, kept frozen for twelve months before it is sold in another hemisphere. This year there is not a plentiful harvest, but an adequate one, and I will not remove myself from the land's energy or that truth.

The crops struggled and the plants wilted in the dry heat, but the life in the earth is still strong. I share cakes and wine in joyful celebration with the other witches, and smile. The fertile power will survive each winter; the God's horns are a promise of it.

I'm going to go off on a tangent for a minute, because I can't really talk about how this deity is perceived in Britain today without mentioning one particular thing. When the modern generation of neo-pagans in the UK are asked which books or other sources inspired them to first look into Paganism, they usually mention at least one of the following three (often with great embarrassment, since many people are now in traditions with very different approaches and these sources are hardly representative of most paganism!). You can try this at any public pagan event, and I've found the same answers coming up every time in the UK.

The three most often quoted are:

"Spiral Dance", a groundbreaking and emotive book on feminist witchcraft by Starhawk,

"The Mists of Avalon", an Arthurian feminist novel focusing on the Goddess, by Marion Zimmer Bradley, and

"Robin of Sherwood", a Robin Hood television series.

It is absolutely astonishing just how well-known and loved this last entry, a 1983 TV show, was (and still is, since the DVDs recently went straight to number 1.) For those who haven't seen it, Robin is especially chosen and favoured by the spirit of the Forest (*'Herne the Hunter'*, appearing as a Stag-headed man). The Sheriff of Nottingham and the Normans are of course Christian.

What was remarkable about the series was the religious element: for the first time ever, a Horned God was shown being worshipped on UK television at 6pm... and he was the good guy! Robin's men gathered in the forest and passed a cup between them, each holding it up and saying *"Herne protect us."* The series (which was packed with occult references – Satanists, Kabbalah, Enchantments, Witches) had *'Herne'* proclaim to Robin: "The powers of light *and* darkness are with you...." It showed a horned animalistic God as the benevolent protector of a loving community of heroes, a band of pagans who were at one with the forest. It opened up to many the idea that the forest could be a holy place at all: the characters' church was a woodland glade, their shrine a sacred oak. It was literally the first time that most of the public saw that a pagan path could be not only free from 'evil', but form a joyful, warm and loving community.

In a way, this is what I hope people get from this book. To the 99% of the general public who do not know anything about this pagan deity, *"The Horned God of the Witches"* means only one well-known guy who lives somewhere hot. I'd love it if this collection of essays and experiences changed that for even a few people. So the TV series was very successful, and continued to be popular for many years. Sure, the synthesiser music stayed in the 80's and the haircuts were fairly tragic... but you can't have everything. The iconic figure of Herne was presented in such a way that it felt instinctively right to many people who would go on to find a pagan path for themselves.

Naturally Mary Whitehouse went berserk. For anyone lucky enough not to know who she was, Mary was the self-appointed guardian of the nation's morals: anything violent or sexy or immoral (and yes, such non-Christian religions or anti-Christian messages really were that racy in 1983) shouldn't be on television where they might harm our children. So she was going to have it censored. Basically, the pagan element was a shockingly different and unexpected theme to be broadcasting at dinner-time.

The reason that I'm mentioning television at all in an otherwise serious essay on personal contact with deity is because that series just would not go away when I sat down to write. The key fact for me is this: the version of "*Herne*" in the show doesn't have a human face. Instead, a man puts on the Stag's head and "*becomes*" the God in a shamanic fashion. He also sends Robin visions and predicts the future, and the line between the man and the God is blurred often during the series. I found myself coming back again and again to the idea of a full stag head, which is why I was surprised when I learnt that the writer said the costume was not originally meant to be an animal head at all – just antlers worn by a human man.

Candlelight flickered on the pentacle, the chalice and other tools on the altar, casting half-shadows onto bare wall behind it. Those two points of flame transformed the room, sent the dull gleam of metal and warm wooden colours out into the darker corners behind me. There were statues of the God and Goddess on either end of the table, but the candles themselves were also representations of them – as I lifted my hands and asked to the Goddess to join me in the night's ritual, my eyes focused on the flame of her candle. I felt her essence like bright colours, and when the small point of light seemed to be all I could see, it was as though only she existed in the World. I bathed in the feelings she created in me. By concentrating on this tiny fire when I called to her, naming her titles and qualities, I felt as though she was in the circle and speaking silently to me.

Next I turned to the second candle. It was the same shape and colour as the first, but felt completely different now that I addressed the God. Again the sensation of his attributes flooded the Universe until they were all there was. I explored them and found that I was rejoicing: it felt very right that these were the forces that the world rested on daily, alongside those of the Goddess. I had no fixed visual image in my mind, but the qualities I called out were different to hers even when some words were the same. 'Strength' meant male strength - solid, dependable, loving support to others. I praised his passion and determination, and ancient connection to the seasons.

I was used to feeling the heavy vitality of the God, but that night his presence was different. His physical strength was less, the deep wordless wisdom replaced with sharp intelligence. This was a human figure who was articulate and aware, a God of magic; the sense of being the male force of nature was still there, but the touch was much lighter and more precise. The mighty power behind it was undiminished. A face appeared in my mind to fit this mix of qualities, one I had never seen before but that expressed the new personality totally. The antlers were not enormous and powerful, part of a connected creature, but smaller. They were a headdress worn by a man who knowingly took on the responsibility for them, and who had the power to fill the role. His eyes glittered with his courage and purpose.

I had no doubt that it was the same deity – but an aspect of him I had not encountered previously. Working with a deity of multiple aspects had been challenging at first (the shining child was the same God as the rampant King?) but this was an experience that would add to my knowledge of him and I was confident that the contact was genuine. I welcomed him to the circle.

The wearing of horns, or symbolic use of them in other ways, has continued in local folk customs until recent times. They are used to signify many of the Horned God's traditional attributes, particularly Kingship, fertility and strength. While there wasn't one main Horned God worshipped in Britain, there were plenty of smaller ones sharing similar traits – and horns have always had this very precise symbolism.

So in some versions of the image we have a looming presence with a Stag head, a towering antlered silhouette, the man completely subsumed by the deity. This is where it impacted most on me: I often find it difficult to picture the Horned God as merely an antlered man instead of something more animalistic. By contrast, I (and others I've asked) often find it easy to see the Goddess with a clear human face.

Should the God have a human face? The original *"Herne"* is either Shakespeare's huntsman from the *Merry Wives of Windsor* (a man with horns affixed to his head) or a name based on the 'Cern' of Cernunnos. Even if we take Cernunnos to be the figure represented on the Gundestrup cauldron (and that's a very contested issue) this is still a human figure with antlers and not a half-animal. Statues for the Wiccan market often try to depict The Horned God as a man who just happens to have whacky headgear, but all too often end up with hilarious *'Jesus'* beards and a gently benevolent expression, or other bizarre image choices. I gave up trying to find a satisfactory statue for my own altar – the only one that I've ever been happy with was made by a friend!

I think this is the heart of it for me. I find it very difficult indeed to include the Horned God in artwork, because the face is never 'right'. I can strongly and instantly feel the general force of him, but putting emotions or personality to it seems to be like trying to staple a Hallowe'en mask on charging stag, or a rumbling thunderstorm. In one altar-piece I made, this feeling was so strong that I ended up drawing nothing but an outlined silhouette. And yet I don't feel this puts any distance into my experience of him, which is often intense.

There aren't many other places to turn to for ideas. The God makes very few other appearances in popular culture: John Masefield's *"The Box of Delights"* features *"Herne the Hunter"* (and that was made into a BBC series in the Eighties too), he appears briefly as a figure with a mix of animalistic features in Susan Cooper's *"The Dark is Rising"* sequence, and Gwyn Ap Nudd is roughly sketched as the adversary in *The Black Cauldron*... but other visual sources for a Cernunnos-like figure are rare. (Comparing this list to the places were a Goddess shows up in popular culture is interesting.)

So I'd looked at his connections with Forests and the Sun, and with Horns, but there was one last area that might help. As a separate exercise I was trying to write rituals for a Men's Mysteries group. Now the fact is, no-one really knows what *'men's mysteries'* involve. You can go the classic route of getting everyone painted in woad to run around a forest carrying torches, but is that really exploring what it is to be essentially male? (Quiet, all of you saying *'yes!'*) Get a women's mysteries group together – even a non-pagan one with members of the public – and if you say you will be working with *"the Goddess"* everyone immediately has roughly the same image in their mind. You just can't do that for a male deity. *"God"* is already someone specific to most people in the UK, and *"not that one"* is not enough of a description to work with. Once again though, we can look at maleness and see what it tells us about the Horned God. The first answer to emerge was, surprisingly, *'mortality'*.

The Goddess may be eternal, but the Horned God dies. A lot.

The mysteries work could have been completely irrelevant to my search for this deity, but it actually helped me. Roles such as Hunter, Warrior, King, Trickster, Blacksmith, Bard, Healer… by looking for what was universally male in these, we can see if any of the attributes seem to fit the God.

We can decide whether a Hunter is strong of arm and fearlessly charging his prey, or a silent and patient archer, full of empathy to predict a deer's behaviour and respect for the life he takes. Whether a Warrior is the person who is best at killing his enemies, or someone who walks a tightrope of honour to keep the respect of his community and not be seen as a danger to all. Again and again the answers refused to be easy. Even the categories were meaningless – female warriors are just as fearsome (and often more ruthless) than males, and female violence is different but undeniably present.

"The Horned God" isn't necessarily connected to all these aspects of maleness, but horns do give him a strong link to the role of King, and in myth that means Sacrifice. Having a King serve for a time and then ritually killing him is a common idea. We see it in nature too: the green trees eventually become bare, the sun retreats… this is a figure whose power clearly wanes. At harvest time, the last of the wheat to be cut is usually referred to as male, and small rituals would be performed to sacrifice it (ensuring life for the next year). John Barleycorn is an example of this idea. I don't think we can ever separate the deity from this cycle: he has many eternal aspects (as the Lord of Death, or one that travels to the Underworld instead of dying) but the strength and animalistic vigour always keep him linked to the idea of losing life.

Ironically, the only thing most people agree that Men's Mysteries always have is a Goddess. This is especially true of Kings. In some cultures (and myth), the King was directly linked to the health of the land because of his role as consort to the Goddess. In others, quests are for the symbol that will lead to completeness, or the unknowable mystery. The Goddess features constantly, and looking at the Horned God without including his position next to Her is never going to give you the whole story.

While that may be a Wiccan view, the deity I'm discussing isn't solely Wiccan. This book is for everyone who wants to discover more about a wider definition of the God: his enduring presence crossing centuries and national borders means that the answers are not limited to any one religion. Therefore, I think the huge scope of his role gives us a duty to experiment widely. We need to walk around outside the book definitions and crafted images every time we explore a new deity (or work more deeply with one for several years!)

In the end, the greatest contribution to how I perceive him came not from looking at any themes or associations, but by doing the work. To anyone reading this, I hope I've given you some ideas. The best way you can take them forward is to finish reading this book, and then just do it. I'm expecting each chapter will be very different because peoples' experience is so subjective, and in the end only how he appears to you will count for anything. Three seconds of communion with a deity may leave you with a different impression. (If your horned god is Woden leading the Wild Hunt, it's likely to be very different!)

I don't just feel him in the determination of the returning greenery in Spring, the nettles and leaves carpeting the forest, the solid resistance of the Oak and noise of the chase... these are some traditional symbols, but he is not always the high energy of the Sun at noon. For me he is there in some less quoted places as well: the beauty of the Dawn, and the wet smells of calmed woodland in Autumn.

This is a difference from my previous experiences with religion. The God (and Goddess) are visibly manifest in nature, every day. In a way, they are the turning of the seasons. My church has become something I carry with me every time I see budding flowers, or vibrant greenery, or bare branches in snow.

"If we do not go to church so much as did our fathers, we go to the woods much more, and are much more inclined to make a temple of them than they were. (Nature) is a power that we can see and touch and hear, and realize every moment of our lives how absolutely we are dependent upon it. There are no atheists or sceptics in regard to this power."
- John Burroughs, 'Time and change' 1912 -

Despite knowing that some pagans use the Horned God as a construct to represent the entire male side of nature, at the same time he also exists as an individual deity. The years pass and my practice evolves, but the depth of my wonder and joy at his gifts has not lessened at all – in his ways he is infinite, and endless, and glorious.

The thick forest is hot and dark. It's late Summer, but that's no guarantee of the weather these days so I'm just thankful it's not frosty or hailing. My brown cloak is heavy over my shoulders, and the Sun on the horizon throws a half-light up into the approaching dusk. There's no chance of being disturbed here, even the most dedicated dog-walkers don't come this far in.

I've been chanting and dancing for what feels like hours, on top of fasting since yesterday. The rhythm has become the heartbeat of the woods. I can feel it now, through my whole body. My legs stamp in time to it, the air breathes in and out with me as I twist and step in a circle around the clearing. This wide ring of trees is the boundary of the whole world.

His presence is everywhere. It lends strength to my muscles, I feel a vast power in my chest. The Holly staff in my right hand thumps the ground and I whip it to the left across my body, and back again. The energy is rising now. Soon it'll be too much to contain – I can sense the weight of trees stubbornly resisting the elements year on year, alongside the heat and emotion of the Horned God ready for the Hunt.

The horns are a crown, a symbol of his worthiness as King, bestowed by the Goddess. They have unconquerable might, but are also a proof of his being one with the land. I am not him, but I wear the horns. They rise up to the sky, and their authority reaches down into the earth. They are much heavier than the antler they are made of, and make me much more than their wearer.

The Horned God is here watching the circle – I see his figure in the shadows now, as always with a sense of the emotions that are in his face but no details. The air is warm, and I quickly throw off my cloak.

I dance once more. When I move my hand, the land moves with it. The weight of mountains are behind my fist. I have spread my palms on the deep earth beneath me and felt the living truth that surrounds us.

Now that weight is rising. He is with me in the clearing, but is impatient to be running, to chase through his domain. The world shakes as he stamps his foot in time with mine, and throws his head back to bellow.

It builds. The weight behind me, increasing like a wave as I look down to the forest floor. In the clearing there is little to see, but on the edge of it the narrow path is a mess of fallen branches and twisted roots. I feel out towards it, becoming one with the tangled undergrowth, getting ready.

It builds. The energy is endless and flowing, a euphoric Sun's glory in my chest. As it approaches the point where the air itself feels charged and saturated, my senses clear and everything shrinks to a bright point above the boiling waves of energy. I reach out, and – claim it.

I run. Hitting the thick tangles with feet made of lightning, I race with the God into the darkness. Trees shoot by on either side, the ground is hidden by a carpet of ivy and nettles but my step is precise and I don't slow at all. We fly along paths and I jump over fallen trunks with my staff held level at my side, shouting for joy at the fire in my body. Pulsing energy radiates from both hands, races up my spine.

It's barely light enough to see now, but I can feel the woodland floor before I reach it. I run and run, one with the forest, and the wild joy of the God flows through me.

DANCING WITH BULLS

By Zagreus

Having grown up on a farm, I have always been intrigued by the power of the bull as a sacred animal. The bull god is one of the earliest of all of man's benefactors, and always fascinated me far more than antlered gods. This fascination has never left me, and has been the focus of my travels around the world. From Knossos to Mysore, from London to Paris, the dance of the bull has always provided me with fresh insights and ideas, and given me the unquenchable power of the bull to draw on.

All journeys have a beginning, and my journey following in the mighty hooves of the bull god could perhaps be said to have started when I read the novel *The Winged Bull* by Dion Fortune as a teenager. I had found a tatty old paperback copy in my local bookshop and decided to try it, intrigued by the by-line that Dion Fortune was *'Mistress of Ritual Magic'*. By such small curiosities are our lives sometimes shaped.

I was absorbed by the book, and when the hero Murchison had his epiphany at the beginning of the novel during his communion with the giant winged bull statue in the British Museum (London), I was moved. I resolved to visit the British

Museum as soon as possible to meet these wondrous beasts for myself. The awesome yet calm might of the statues, just as evoked by Fortune in her prose, gave form to my admiration for the mighty bull, and made me determined to find out more.

I was given the chance by a school trip to Paris. We went to the Louvre, and after much wheedling and cajoling I managed to persuade one of the teachers to help me find the Sumerian statues there. Again I encountered the winged bull, and an even more intriguing image, the bull-horned king as god, rather than the man-headed bull. The Victory Stele of king Naram-Sin shows him wearing a horned helmet, and leading his troops to victory. Such a helmet clearly indicated that the king was acting as the avatar of the mighty bull god of Sumer, Enlil, in battle, and was a vessel for that mighty force to be transferred to his army, ensuring victory in battle. As I learned, the bull god was an ongoing tradition in ancient Sumeria and Mesopotamia. The bull god of Ur, Nannar, was described as *'heavenly lord'*, *'moon god'* and *'lord of the brilliant crescent'*. The link between the moon and the bull was clearly established in my mind by this. Interestingly as society changed, so too did the attribution of the bull to the might of the sun rather than the moon. Thus Marduk, in taking over from Enlil as the dominant god, was a solar bull rather than an earthly one with lunar connections. His name means *'young steer of the day'*, clearly indicating his solar bull nature. From here the source of the bull horned solar disk seen worn by the goddess Hathor and other Egyptian deities seems clear.

The solar bull was also found on Crete, with the highly successful sea-based Minoan culture of antiquity. The worship of the solar bull, with its bull dances, fights and sacrifices have become immortalised in the myth of Theseus in the image of the minotaur, the bull-headed man guarding the sacred labyrinth under the palace, a secret shame or hidden god depending on your viewpoint.

Unlike the modern Spanish bullfighters who display their *'manhood'* through taunting bulls weakened by numerous spears and with their neck tendons cut to prevent them even looking up, the Cretan youths performed their acrobatic leaps over the bull's backs in the full knowledge that they might be gored or trampled if their timing was out. It was a contest of skill which pushed the athletes to the limit. Whilst I was staying in Knossos some years back, I had a dream of being one such athlete around three and a half thousand years ago. In my dream I stood waiting for the charging bull, my heart racing as it drew ever closer. At the last moment as it lowered its horns I grasped them and somersaulted forwards, over its mighty head, landing on its back and then jumping off onto the ground as it snorted forwards. With every successful somersault my standing grew, as more of the magickal power of the bull was transferred to me through the horns. As the dream was ended by the sound of cockerels from outside, it had changed, and I was the bull, charging at myself. The message of my dream was clear, testing yourself is all well and good, but be sure you know who you are first.

My next step in the dance of the bull, having leaped through the labyrinth of Knossos, was to visit India, home of the mighty Nandi Bull, avatar of the god Shiva. I travelled to India, booking a package holiday to Goa, and then making my way by train to Mysore. The walk up Chamundi hill to the temple at the top was an unmissable experience. I felt I had to stop at each of the little shrines that had been built, which meant that the journey ended up taking about five times as long as it would if I had just walked straight to the top. I also managed to cut my hand on one of the small shrines, which was I think to Parvati or another such Indian goddess. I thought it was Parvati as she is the Lady of the Mountain and wife of Shiva, but it was hard to tell, as it was just a simple statue with a shiva lingam and some flowers. Burning some sandalwood joss purchased from one of the vendors at the bottom of the hill, I drew a trident in the air in honour of Shiva and somehow cut the side of my palm on a sharp stone I hadn't noticed.

Whilst I was paying my respects to the giant statue of the Nandi Bull at the Sri Chamundeswari Temple on top of the hill, one of the priests noticed my bleeding hand and enquired about it. I explained about the shrine, and he decided it was obviously a sign and he had to take me in hand. Grabbing me by the arm he pulled me to where the huge stone shiva lingams stood proud. Amazingly there was nobody else around, and he left me standing contemplating the scale and symbolism of the Shiva lingam, before quickly returning. After telling me to copy his actions, he encouraged me to light cones of camphor, and then pour milk into the lip of the Shiva lingams. We sat and chanted mantra for a while, and then he led me back to the Nandi Bull. Ignoring the crowd, he took me under the rope to stand directly next to Nandi's right front leg. He told me to draw a pair of bull horns on the leg with my blood, and I noticed how up close the stone had been discoloured over the years by the amount of oil that had been rubbed into it by faithful devotees. To this I added my blood, and felt a tremendous sense of power flow from the huge statue into me. For the first time in my life I gained a sense of how much power could be stored in a statue by the belief of worshippers.

The next stage of my journey, which has now reached that moment of feeling imminent, will be travelling to Egypt. I also want to go to Iraq to see some of the sites and antiquities there, but I think I will be waiting a few years for that one. Though who knows, the bull god has a way of leading you into steps of the dance you never thought you could make. Perhaps my next journey will be closer to home on the trail of the Celtic bull-horned gods that have started to call me.

MEDITATION JOURNEY WITH GWYNN AP NUDD

BY GARETH GERRARD

Sit in a quiet place with eyes closed and spend a few minutes relaxing and being aware of your breathing. In your mind's eye, visualise your immediate surroundings and see a white, all-encompassing mist rise up and completely surround you. The mist thins and you find yourself on the edge of a large forest; it is dusk and a large full moon hangs low above the horizon. You see a worn path that leads into the forest; follow it and head towards the dark, forbidding woods. As you enter the forest, you pass between two ancient hawthorn tree, gnarled and interlocked. Continue to follow the path, passing deeper and deeper into the woods.

The forest is quiet, apart from the gentle rustle of the wind in the leaves and the occasional scurrying of small animals in the undergrowth flanking the path. You are aware of your breathing and the sound of your footsteps on the old, worn path. From the distance behind you, just on the edge of your awareness, you hear the unmistakable baying of hounds; wild and mournful. They are hunting. Your pulse quickens as you realise they are heading your way; quickly, increase your pace and head further into the forest.

The terrible sound of the spectral hounds grows closer and closer. You are running now; running for your life. Your feet are fleet and swift as you rush headlong into the gloaming, pale grey branches and dark clouds of undergrowth blur as you speed down the twisting path towards the heart of the forest.

Your speed is to no avail; the baying grows ever closer, no matter how fast you run. Your feet seem to barely skim the rough path and the hounds, relentless in their pursuit, are almost upon you. Through the fear, you feel a pulse of exhilaration; through running for your life, you feel what it is to be alive, and you realise that even though you rush headlong through a dark forest, no branch impedes you and no roots catch your feet: you are fleet and agile and at one with your environment.

The hounds are upon you, but instead of biting jaws and tearing flesh, you feel that your feet no longer seem to touch the ground. You look down and find yourself no longer upon the path, but heading up between dark branches into the now night sky, rushing above the moonlit canopy. Around you are the Cŵn Annwfn – ghostly white bodies with eyes and ears as red as blood. You run with them, the wild hunt, howling triumphant as you skim the tree tops, heading ever towards the heart of the forest.

Suddenly, they lead you back beneath the leafy canopy, diving down through a rush of bough and branch, and onto the soft grass of a large clearing. An open fire burns brightly at the centre, and the hounds cease their baying and sit and gaze at the fire with excited expectation.

You walk towards the fire, and in the flickering ruddy light, you realise that you can make out the shape of a large man sitting cross legged on ground. He gestures for you to join him and you sit. His eyes are piercingly bright in his dark face, and his wild hair is held back by a simple silver circlet. His clothes are simple and travel worn, finished by a grey woollen cloak. His demeanour is powerful and regal.

He says that you have been hunted by the Cŵn Annwfn and that they have brought you to him. In order to return to your own world you must first forfeit to him a part of yourself. Since his is the escort to the grave, consider some negative, outmoded or hindering aspect of yourself, which you would like to leave behind, and visualise it as a small object or symbol. See this representation of the negative aspect of yourself in your hand and give it to him. He holds it up to the light of the flames and considers it briefly before placing it in the heart of the blazing fire, where it disperses in a shower of sparks.

Spend a few moments in silent contemplation before thanking Gwynn ap Nudd and walking back, through the pack of Cŵn Annwfn, who regard you interest, but let you pass unhindered. You find the path at the opposite end of the clearing and notice that the first light of dawn is brightening through the trees. Follow the golden lit path towards the rising sun until you find yourself back at the guardian hawthorn trees, which you pass through and find yourself back where you started. You look back at the forest and you notice a mist begin to rise up and obscure your vision. And then, as it clears, you find yourself back in your own body, sitting with your eyes closed. Take three deep breaths and open your eyes.

HYMN TO AMEN-RA

Hymn to Amen-Ra, the Bull in Heliopolis,
President of all the gods,
Beneficent god, beloved one,
The giver of warmth of life to all beautiful cattle,
Hail to thee, Amen-Ra,
Lord of the thrones of Thebes,
Bull of his mother,
Chief of his fields
Lord of the sky,
Eldest son of the earth,
Lord of the things which exist,
Establisher of things,
Establisher of all things,
One in his time among the gods,
Beautiful Bull of the company of the gods,
Father of the gods,
Maker of men,
Creator of beasts and cattle,
Lord of the things which exist,
Master of the herbage whereon cattle live,
Form made by Ptah,
Beautiful child
Beloved one.

(From Fetish to God in Ancient Egypt, Budge, 1934)

JOURNEY TO THE MOUND

BY GULIA LAINI

Sit cross legged on the floor with your back straight, making sure you are comfortable, and relax. Focus on your breathing and the air entering and leaving your nostrils. As you breathe and relax more, in your mind's eye see yourself sitting as you are. Fix the image of yourself sitting in the room in your mind's eye. Now as you see yourself sitting in the room, see a white mist starting to form, filling the room. The mist becomes thicker and thicker, obscuring the walls, the floor, the ceilings, until all around you is white mist, you are floating in a sea of white mist.

The white mist starts to disperse, and as it does so you smell the deep earthy and woody smell of a forest all around you. You look around and through the foliage of the wood you see the golden rays of the setting sun casting a golden glow through the clearing you are standing in. The shapes of oak and ash and hawthorn trees edge the clearing, and from the white blossoms on the hawthorns you realise that it must be May, the time of Beltane.

Continuing to study your surroundings, you see a glimpse of movement by a path on the far side of the clearing. A patch of red and white catches your eye and you realise it is a magnificent stag.

It bounds off into the forest and you hurry after it, running across the clearing and down the path that tracks through the woods. The golden glow of the setting sun is tinged with pink, filling the woods with a fiery glow and making them look like they are burning with an ethereal flame.

You glimpse the stag in the distance and continue your pursuit, and as you run the forest starts to come more alive around you. You hear the barking of foxes in the distance, and an owl hoots nearby. The hunters are coming out, and you realise that you are one of their number. With a burst of speed you sprint forward and enter a grove, where the grass is all short, and in the centre is a large mound with a stone entrance way into the darkness. You see the tail of the stag as it bounds into the mound, and you follow.

As you enter the passageway into the mound you feel a moisture in the air, and you see a dripping portal ahead. The stone arch in front of you drips constantly, producing a translucent sheet of water. You step through this watery doorway and into a large circular chamber, lit by a central fire. There is no sign of the stag, but as you look around you see there are carvings of animals on the stones in the walls. Stags and wolves, boars and bears, foxes and badgers, hares and salmon, eagles and owls, they are all etched into the large stones. The floor is packed earth beneath your feet, and the ceiling is flat overhead, as the huge capstone separates you from the grass and earth on top of the mound.

You return your gaze to the fire in the centre of the chamber. You step closer, and feel its heat drying the water off you. As you stare at the ferocious flames, you notice there is no wood feeding them, and that they seem to shoot up directly from the earth. As you realise this a figure starts to form in the flames. You see antlers, and then a strong and proud face beneath the antlers, and broad shoulders, as the horned god manifests through the fire, steeping through the flames like a doorway. He wears a simple skin breechclout, and has golden torcs around his wrists. Curled around his left hand is a snake, with bright eyes and small ram horns protruding from its brow.

He opens his right hand and for a moment you think you see the golden glow of the sun there, but then it is gone and you see his hand is empty. The horned god gestures and you stand in front of the carving which draws you most. You look at his face and realise the antlers of the stag you chased were identical to his, and that from hunter you are now prey. His face reminds you of a bird of prey, ready to swoop onto its prey. Nervously you look deep into the fierce eyes and you see them soften with humour as he laughs.

You laugh too, realising that he has made his hunt and been successful, now he is guardian of the land, both above and below. At this realisation the room suddenly shines with a golden light, as the carvings in the stone give out a golden light, as they all suddenly seem to come to life with a vibrant power. You turn and touch the carving of your beast, and feel some of the golden power flow into your hand and into your body. Invigorated you turn around and face the horned god again.

Now you see he looks different, and you notice that where his skin had seemed dark, it was in fact fine tattoos of leaves, and some of these are now fading as his skin shines with a golden luminescence. Those that do not fade seem to become more verdant and alive, and the green and gold glow from his body is almost overpowering. He steps back into the fire, the flames licking all around him. As he starts to disappear in the flames he throws something to you. He fades from view and you look in your hand at the silver coin he threw to you. On one side is a stag, and the other side as you turn it over is so smooth and blank it acts as a mirror and you see yourself reflected in it. Holding on to the coin firmly, you look around the chamber once more, and as you do so you notice the flames are dying down and the chamber is filling with a white mist. The mist is becoming more and more dense, obscuring the walls, the floor, the ceiling, the dying fire, until all around you is white mist. You are surrounded by white mist. And now the mist starts to disperse, and as it does so you see yourself sitting once more in your room. As the last of the mist fades away, take a deep breath, open your eyes and readjust yourself to your surroundings.

THE FIRE HORNS
By Lupus

I am the wolf that howls from the wild
I am the sun reborn as a child
I am the face that peers from the leaves
I am the corn you gather in sheaves
I am the fire in every hearth
I am the sorrow in every laugh
I am the shadow returned to the womb
I am the comet whose tail brings doom
I am the carrion crow plucking an eye
I am the mirror that tells no lie
I am the horns seen from afar
I am the spark that burns in each star
I am the dance of the wind and the rain
I am the cloak that comforts the pain
I am the spirit that prompts you to grow
The question whose answer you already know.
I am you and you are me
The flow of magick wild and free

Horns of Beauty

Horned Goddesses

LUNA'S SHINING HORNS

BY GULIA LAINI

The Moon is one of the most represented and revered bodies in the night sky, one of the Great Luminaries shining down on Earth brightly and in constant flux. Sometimes she is the full beauty and mystery of the Full Moon and at other times she shines down as a sliver of light, the crescent Moon. It is the crescent shape which has most often been associated with both male and female lunar deities from around the world. There is some evidence that in some instances, the crescent shape adorning the brows of ancient Gods and Goddesses are in fact symbolic depictions of animal horns. The animal horns in time made place for the more civilised and discrete symbolic horns in the shape of the crescent Moon, a symbol of grace and beauty, and of tremendous magickal power. After all, magick and mystery have always been associated with the ever-changing shape of the Moon.

The lunar horns are associated with both male and female divinities, and in fact, in most cultures the Moon is personified as a male divinity, not a female one. Thus the symbol of the horns of the Moon is associated with deities as far apart as the Egyptian Thoth, the Hindu Shiva through to the Roman Luna and Diana, Greek

Selene, Hekate and Artemis, as well as the Sumerian Sin and the Japanese Tsukiyomi.

The development of horns into the lunar crescent can be seen with the god Shiva. In the early Harappan culture in the Indus Valley c. 3000 BCE was a horned god called Pashupati, whose name means *Lord of the Beasts*. This god is also known as proto-Shiva, as he developed into Shiva. Thus we see the antlers becoming the upward pointing crescent. It is not hard to imagine other horns becoming more subtle and graceful crescents which moved away from the more animalistic past to a more upward looking lunar and stellar future.

In some instances the lunar associations are directly linked to horned animals, such as in the following passage from the *Orphic Hymn to Selene*:

"To Selene (Moon), Fumigation from Aromatics. Hear, goddess queen, diffusing silver light, bull-horned, and wandering through the gloom of night. With stars surrounded, and with circuit wide night's torch extending, through the heavens you ride..."

To the ancient Greeks Selene was the personification of the Moon. She was the Goddess of the Moon who rode upon a silver chariot through the night sky, just like Helios (the Sun God) rode through the day sky on his golden chariot. Her status as a Horned Goddess is emphasised in writings such as that of the Greek Epic, Nonnus' *Dionysiaca*: "*Give me best, Selene, horned driver of cattle! Now I am both - I have horns and I ride a bull!' So he called out boasting to the round Moon.*" This story inevitably ends up in a gory mess, as a lesson to those who think they can taunt a Goddess. Ampelos (the love of Dionysus) ends up gorged to death by a bull as a result of his boasting, illustrating how horns associated with a Goddess are by no means gentle or otherwise inferior in power to the horns of male divinities.   They are still horns of power, symbols of the inherent power held by that divinity – be it physical or magickal.

This is clear when we consider one of the most famous horned goddesses of all time, the Egyptian Mother Goddess Isis. In later depictions of Isis she is shown with horns adorning either side of the sundisk she wears as the daughter of Ra. The horns were originally associated with the cow goddess Hathor, but in the later kingdom when Isis assumed more powers she also became associated with the Moon; as well as taking on the title of Mistress of Magick by having tricked the sun god Ra's power from him by gaining his true name. Isis is also shown throughout the entire Egyptian kingdom as being associated with kingship, in fact her name Isis (sometimes said as Aset or Isa) can be taken to mean '*The Throne*'. Again this clearly demonstrates that horns when associated with the feminine divine are often symbols associated with particularly powerful goddesses.   As I briefly mentioned the cow goddess Hathor, it might be worth exploring her nature here too.

Hathor was often referred to as the eye of Ra and was considered to be the beautiful goddess, with power over sexuality and motherhood. She had particular talents over music, song and dance, as well as drunkenness and the female reproductive organs. The colour red, associated in Egypt with power, was connected with Hathor as the Mistress of the Red Cloth. She was also the protectress of endeavours in foreign lands, such as mining metals and minerals, and of these the turquoise was particularly sacred to her.   Hathor was also associated with protecting children, in a multiple form called the Seven Hathors. Knotted red ribbons sacred to Hathor were used for both protecting expectant mothers and also to bind dangerous spirits and poisons. Her horned disk combined day and night, with the sun surrounded by the lunar horns, and she was also sometimes referred to as Lady of the Stars.

In the Middle Ages the horned goddess with her lunar crescent returned in the imagery of the alchemists. She was snow-white Diana, the crowned huntress queen wearing the lunar crescent, the white stone which transmutes all into the finest silver and balances the power of the red stone. Diana of the silver moon-tree, which bore itself as fruit, every twisted branch another pattern of horns. Her moon-tree reminds us that it is not only horns which are shared by goddesses and gods.

So what do Luna's shining horns teach us? They teach us that everything is in flux, and nothing should be taken for granted. Even the things we are told must be questioned, lest we become too accepting and lose our way by taking our eyes off the path, the path lit by those horns of power shining bright.

Bibliography
Athanassakis, A.; *The Orphic Hymns: Text, Translation & Notes*; 1988; Society of Biblical Literature; Atlanta
Nonnus; *Dionysiaca Books 1-15*; 1965; Harvard University Press
Watterson, Barbara; *The Gods of Ancient Egypt*; 1984; Batsford; London

TRIPLE HORNS OF THE GREEK MAGICAL PAPYRI

BY SORITA D'ESTE

During my research on the Greek goddesses Hekate and Artemis for the books I edited and wrote on them, as well as for my personal work over the years, I have repeatedly encountered the *Greek Magical Papyri*. This collection of hymns, magical formulae, rituals and spells from Greco-Roman Egypt of 2nd century BCE – 5th century CE is an amazing collection of material which not only provides a wealth of insights into that world at that time, but also has a lot of useful material that can be drawn upon for modern magickal work.

The *Greek Magical Papyri* (often abbreviated to PGM) contain reference to a wide range of deities from a number of pantheons, including Greek, Egyptian, Sumerian and Hebrew. However of all the deities mentioned, the most common goddesses are the Greek goddesses Artemis, Hekate and Selene. These goddesses are mentioned to such an extent and so interchangeably that it can be hard to determine which of them is being called on until you appreciate that in many instances the three goddesses are being viewed as a triple goddess.

This conflation of these goddesses had already occurred before the *Greek Magical Papyri* were written. Artemis and Hekate were being equated through their titles, appearance and attributes from the 5th century BCE. Thus both Artemis and Hekate were portrayed as beautiful maidens accompanied by dogs and serpents, and at times wearing short skirts and hunting boots. They shared titles like Enodia (*"of the road"*), Propylaii (*"of the gate"*) and Phosphorus (*"light bringer"*), and the joining of their names in attributes is seen in writings such as those of Aiskhylos who wrote in the fifth century BCE in Suppliants, *"that Artemis-Hekate watch over the childbed of their women."*

Artemis and Selene were both frequently identified with each other as lunar goddesses from the 2nd century BCE onwards. The Greek *Lyric Fragments* describe how, *"Artemis is Selene"*, an attitude which carries on into the *Greek Magical Papyri*. As Artemis was equated to both Selene and Hekate, it is not surprising that these latter two goddesses should also be equated. Thus by the end of the period covered by the *Greek Magical Papyri*, in the 5th century CE we see Nonnus in his *Dionysiaca* writing: *"O Selene, driver of the silver chariot! If thou art Hekate of many names ... if thou art staghunter Artemis ..."*

Indeed some researchers are now going as far as to say this interconnection of goddesses also includes Persephone and Mene, as can be seen by Kotansky in *Antiquity and Humanity: Essays on Ancient Religion and Philosophy* where he writes:

"By the time of the writing of the Greek Magical Papyri, in fact, Artemis-Hekate-Selene-Mene-Persephone were so intimately intertwined that any differentiation between them as archetypal moon goddesses and earthly, netherworld figures was impossible."

As I have read the prayers and incantations of the *Greek Magical Papyri*, I have been struck by the number of times this triplicity of goddesses is referred to in connection with horns, as horned goddesses. It is common practice to associate bull horns, which have a long association with power, to gods such as Serapis and Zeus, but not generally to goddesses. Considering the references are there in plain view, is this an oversight, or a preference to put things into convenient boxes for labelling?

Working through the *Greek Magical Papyri*, there are six significant lines I wish to discuss, three of which come from one invocation, and two of which refer to engraving on gemstones, a common ancient practice.

Three of the references come from a *Prayer to Selene for Any Spell* (PGM IV.2785-2890). In the rubric of this prayer the references are specifically to the goddess being bull-headed. Not only is she bull headed, but also bull-faced and bull-eyed. Thus she is:

"Night-Crier, bull-faced, loving solitude, bull-headed, you have eyes of bulls" (PGM IV.2809-10)

We may also note that she is elevated to a more all-encompassing role later in this prayer, which is in keeping with the view of Hekate expressed in the *Chaldean Oracles*, where she is *"the Mistress of Life and holds the plenitude of the full womb of the cosmos"* (Fragment 96). From descriptions of her terrifying and animalistic forms, she has become the Mother of all things:

"bull-eyed, horned, mother of gods and men, and Nature, Mother of all things," (PGM IV.2832-33)

As well as providing the rubric for the charm, the construction and form of the charm is explicitly detailed at the end of the prayer, and leaves us in no doubt who the charm is made for and addressed to. Lodestone, with its magnetic qualities, was particularly popular for charms due to its perceived magickal attractive qualities. It was especially used in Hekate charms. Whilst the nature of the offerings may seem grisly to us today, they would not have seemed so two thousand years ago. The blood of a person who has died violently was considered to be more charged, and it was a common practice to *'feed'* blood and offer food to charms to further imbue them with magickal power.

"Protective charm for the rite: Take a lodestone and on it have carved a three-faced Hekate. And let the middle face be that of a maiden wearing horns, and the left face that of a dog, and the one on the right that of a goat. After the carving is done, clean with natron and water, and dip in the blood of one who has died a violent death. Then make a food offering to it and say the same spell at the time of the ritual." (PGM IV.2880-84)

What is particularly interesting about this charm, apart from its threefold nature, is the faces themselves. The middle face, of the maiden with a human face, shows her wearing horns, presumably indicating the horns of the crescent moon, emphasising her lunar nature and suggesting this face represents Selene. The left face of the dog is clearly of Hekate, as there are numerous references to her in canine form, being called such names as *"Black Bitch"* (PGM IV.1434), and *"dog in maiden form"* (PGM IV.2251). Hekate is also depicted in triple form with the left face as a dog in *Pitys' Spell of Attraction* (PGM IV.2006-2125), where the triformis image is drawn onto a leaf of flax.

The right face is of a goat, an interesting choice as it is not an association seen elsewhere. However that it is in opposition to the dog face reminds us of the pack of hunting dogs given by Pan to Artemis and described in Callimachus' *Hymn to Artemis*. The connection to Artemis may be further indicated by its use as a sacrificial animal in major ceremonies to her. It is believed that goats were sacrificed to Artemis during the Brauronia festival at her major cult centre of Brauron, and the festival of Charisteria, celebrating the Greek victory at Marathon, saw five hundred goats sacrificed to Artemis. On this evidence I feel it is fair to assume that the three faces are, as I have suggested, the dog for Hekate, the maiden for Selene and the goat for Artemis.

The next reference is in a *Spell of Attraction* (PGM IV.2441-2621), where the bull horns are again emphasised. It is interesting to note that she is specifically called *"horned-faced"* here, indicating the horns as part of her, not an attachment. The use of the term light-bringer also returns to the shared titles, being as previously mentioned one used by both Hekate and Artemis:

"Come to me, horned-faced, light-bringer, bull-shaped" (PGM IV.2548-49)

In many pantheons qualities are often shared between daughters and mothers, and this can be seen with the goddess Mene. Mene is the singular of Menai, meaning *'lunar months'*, which was the name of Selene's fifty daughters who she bore to the shepherd Endymion. The fifty daughters correspond to the number of moons in the four year period of an Olympiad, between Olympic Games. The singular name Mene is sometimes used in the *Greek Magical Papyri*, interchangeably with the complex of goddesses we are considering, particularly as a substitute for Selene. Thus we see:

"I call upon you who have all forms and many names, double-horned goddess, Mene" (PGM VII.756-57)

A final reference is the second gem carving, an intriguing image of a snake ouroboros with Selene wearing her lunar crescent, with a star on top of each of its two horns. The snake was a symbol of both Hekate and Artemis, and hence has been transferred to Selene as her emblem by the process of equation of these goddesses. The two stars at the top of the horns might also hint at the threefold nature of Selene in her connection with Artemis and Hekate, being reminiscent of the twin torches of Hekate representing Venus as the morning and evening star.

"Taking an air-coloured jasper, engrave on it a snake in a circle with its tail in its mouth, and also in the middle of the circle formed by the snake Selene having two stars on the two horns." (PGM XII.202-4)

As I have shown through this essay, the lunar crescent and bull horns are both common symbols associated with the three goddesses Artemis, Hekate and Selene in the *Greek Magical Papyri*. That the bull horns should be interchangeable with the lunar crescent seems an obvious link to make. Whether in a stellar form as the Moon or a terrestrial form as the bull, the horns represent the visible power of the lunar goddesses, and this is a point to remember when you consider that this is often only one of their range of powers.

Bibliography
Betz, Hans Dieter; *The Greek Magical Papyri in Translation*; 1992; University of Chicago Press; Chicago
Bonner, C.; *Studies in Magical Amulets, Chiefly Graeco-Egyptian*; 1950; Ann Arbor; Michigan
d'Este, Sorita; *Artemis: Virgin Goddess of the Sun and Moon*; 2005; Avalonia; London
Kotansky, Roy; *Jesus and the Lady of the Abyss: Hieros Gamos, Cosmogony and the Elixir of Life*; in *Antiquity and Humanity: Essays on Ancient Religion and Philosophy*; 2001; Mohr Siebeck
Johnston, Sarah Iles; *Hekate Soteira*; 1990; Scholars Press; Atlanta

ODE TO THE HORNED GODDESS

By Nina Falaise

Silver Horned One, Beauteous One clothed in Gold.
Leaf after leaf sailing softly to the ground,
Kissing the feet of the One who loves you.
Tearful eyes look longingly at a turquoise sky,
She, with piercing gaze, looks upon the human form, lustfully.
Speechless, lost in silent wilderness,
Listening to the shimmering Golden One,
Sweet, sharp voice echoes out,
Singing into the unknown knowingly.
She, holding the Key of Life to the One,
Speaks words of power.
Crisp and fresh, straight from Her sensuous lips,
Seeds thrown from the Great Rattle,
Scatter to the winds of time.
Heavenly Grace, heaving bosom from Earth's beating Heart.
Mother of One and All calling to the One.
Child of Light takes flight,
Meeting the Silver Horned One in Her Kingdom.
Golden One, Beauteous One.
Blue Lotus, head lifted to the Light,
Roots burying beneath murky waters, connecting Heaven to Earth,
In the blood red river of Life....

'Het-Hert – Hathor' painting by Nina Falaise

Invocation of Elen

Horned Lady
Wild Enchantress
Elen, Horned One
To you I call

Horned Lady,
Great Bestower
Of the Mysteries
To my Circle call

Horned Lady
Elen, Huntress
Of the straight-ways
To you I call

Horned Lady
Fast and Quiet
Stalk your prey
Now our journey
Must begin

Words by MDL

IN PURSUIT OF ELEN

By Jenny Sumaya

When I began working with Elen I thought I had a very clear image in my mind. It wasn't, I didn't believe, an image much affected by the Neopagan Elen of the 1980's. The Reindeer Horned, eco-warrior, was an image I'd not really come across. But I did know of Elen as a horned goddess, which in my mind perfectly fitted the Elen of the ways I knew from the folk tales and little myths I read when I grew up in Wales. I can only assume that, at least initially, a passing comment or a sentence taken for granted in a book, had lodged the image of the Horned Elen, firmly in my mind.

When a friend and I started looking deeper into the *'knowledge'* and *'facts'* of Elen we came across a problem, there was practically nothing written down except internet stories and theories, and these could be quite wild and wonderful in some circumstances! But a general picture grew that Elen had *'appeared'* (literally) in the 1980's and was embraced by those connected to her. But where had she come from beforehand? Who had she been? Who was she now, to me?

Tentative links are made to mythical and historical figures from Helen of Troy (probably the least likely association) to Elen of the Ways, but all of them are threads and theories with little 'proof' other than individual beliefs. For example, the association I had made with the Welsh Elen Luyddog is one of the most frequently quoted. Elen is a welsh variant of Helen, and she can be tentatively traced in both myth and history. The myths of Helen of the Hosts, her titles and the *Dream of Mascen Wledig* do seem to describe a deity. But there is little relation to a Horned Goddess, a guardian or animals and nature. The unquestioned association suddenly didn't seem to make any factual sense. But I felt sure of the Horned Goddess; the imagery is not by any means non-existent, but the associations we have so far made for her have come either from non-British sources or from tentative and unlikely links to figures in myth. I realised that I wasn't going to find the Horned Goddess I knew in books.

So now I will speak of personal experience and association, there is no basis in fact or literature for this – though I have tried to find some traces of literature and others experience, before the 1980's that is (as if it becomes more real because it is older?).

First to dispel an assumption that may be made. The image of the Reindeer Horned Elen does not fit well with me. This is just a personal opinion, but if she is truly a Welsh / British deity, what experiences have we of the unknown wastelands of the Siberian deserts of snow and ice. What knowledge have we of the unbelievable treks of the Reindeer and those who depend upon them? For there is only one female Reindeer with those horns, and she can only be found so far north.

So to the Horned Goddess I call Elen (for she does not seem unhappy with the name), and the association I still make with a Welsh Elen. My own personal experience of paths and tracks in Wales are those of the sheep tracks, tracing the easiest paths across the mountains through apparently impassable valleys and bogs. The Roman roads attributed to Elen of the Ways, (Sarn (H)elen) do exist in Wales, they have the unusual distinction of rarely being straight, they also take the easiest route – which in Wales would be the fastest.

I do not, making this faint connection with a name, say that there is any logical reason to make the connection between a Goddess of the safe path, and the Horned Goddess of the wild; no logical connection but perhaps an illogical one.

If it helps, let me describe for you the Horned Goddess, the Elen I have known. She has come in two forms; they are the same, though the appearance is different.

She is not tall, but with the heart of the wildwood, fast, quiet, she is stalker and the prey. In human form she carries a spear, flint tipped and leather bound, but has no more trappings or covering, other than the ever changing patterns in her soft skin. Her eyes are strong and gentle, the deep brown eyes of the roe deer, whose horns she wears. She is fleet of foot, strong and silent. She is nature of human and animal across the moor and in the deep wild forest.

The other, unexpected image, the same beautiful face, the same deep brown eyes, but clothed in a soft hooded robe. She has walked amongst man, she has seen and understands civilisation, she knows the wisdom of words and books, but she brings with her spirit, the depth of nature the greenwoods and the deer. She is still the Horned Goddess, but that part is quiet and still, enabling her to be present in the streets without notice or fear. To bring with her the wild passions of the past without that power being all-consuming. She needs not see them dance on the street, she will take them dancing in dreams.

I have called to her in the wildwood, amid the deer and the ancient trees, and she has led a merry dance. I found her in the search and not in the finding and She has taught me how to find a safe path, She has taught me the song in silence. She is a nature spirit, and something deeper rooted than that. I sought her because of a name and I found that, whereas the name may be right or wrong, the entity is strong still and stronger now perhaps than ever before.

Does this Horned Elen have any place in literature or written 'fact': not to my knowledge. But she is my experience of the Horned Goddess, the Goddess I choose to call Elen.

Ingram Content Group UK Ltd.
Milton Keynes UK
UKHW010651250523
422331UK00001B/5

9 781905 297177